Praise for *Waking in Havana*

"Elena Schwolsky has written to struggle and service. Her stories—from the front lines of the AIDS pandemic—are heartbreaking and profoundly inspirational. From Newark to Havana, Elena shares stories of great poignancy, humor, and deep insight as she evolves from idealistic and passionate young woman to seasoned and practical veteran of the movement. Schwolsky never describes herself as a hero, but she most certainly is one."

—Cleve Jones, author of *When We Rise: My Life in the Movement* and founder of the AIDS Memorial Quilt

"*Waking in Havana* will awaken readers to the extraordinary ways in which cultural bridges can create understanding and reciprocity between Cubans and Americans, even on issues as complex as the AIDS crisis. Elena Schwolsky is a unique 'yuma' in Havana who gives back more than she receives, revealing how Cuba opened her heart in unexpected ways."

—Ruth Behar, Professor of Anthropology, University of Michigan, and author of *Lucky Broken Girl*

"*Waking in Havana* explores territory few dare to tread. Set in turbulent times where Cold War Cuba meets the AIDS crisis, Schwolsky succeeds in crafting a deeply intimate tale of grief and healing—hers and others—while immersed in a foreign (and often contradictory) culture. Schwolsky's memoir probes thorny issues, including survivor's guilt, acculturation, bias, and addiction, through painstaking prose full of the humanity, solidarity, creativity, and humor for which Cubans are known. This firsthand account from the front lines of Cuba's AIDS program is guaranteed to make readers laugh and cry—much like the misunderstood island the author grew to know and love."

—Conner Gorry, author of *100 Places in Cuba Every Woman Should Go* and manager of Cuba Libro, Havana's only English-language bookstore

"Like Elena Schwolsky, I was a nurse in the broken heart of an American city during the 1980s and '90s and witnessed the effects of HIV and AIDS on the families I cared for and the larger community. . . reading this very personal and compelling memoir, I kept thinking of a line from Mary Oliver's poem, "The Summer Day": *Tell me, what is it you plan to do / with your one wild and precious life?* In *Waking in Havana*, Schwolsky tells us what she has done with hers. Trust me, you will want to find out."

—Veneta Masson, RN, MA, author of *Clinician's Guide to the Soul*

"With warmth, humor, and endless compassion, Elena Schwolsky has created a remarkable and timely memoir. *Waking In Havana* brings us intimately along Schwolsky's path to healing from her husband Clarence's death from AIDS, which winds right through the unforgettable world of a 1990s Cuban AIDS sanitarium. This book reinforces the importance of the stories of people that society too often casts aside—not just to prevent others from dehumanizing the most vulnerable but because of how much all of us gain through connecting to each other."

—Aaron Zimmerman, executive director of the NY Writers Coalition and author of *By The Time You Finish This Book You Might Be Dead*

"Elena Schwolsky takes us on an unforgettable journey through the trenches: as an idealistic *Venceremos brigadista* doing her part to build a new nation; a pediatric AIDS nurse on the front lines of the epidemic that claimed her Vietnam veteran husband; and as a grieving widow volunteering at one of Cuba's controversial AIDS sanatoriums, where she inspires the creation of Cuba's first AIDS quilt panel. Her remarkable story bears compassionate witness to the resilience and courage of one of the most vulnerable communities both in the US and in her beloved, quixotic Cuba."

—Mindy Lewis, author of *Life Inside: A Memoir*

"The author's loving descriptions of people whose lives have been directly and intimately impacted by HIV/AIDS humanizes the meaning of this epidemic. It is more than just telling their stories; her rich attention to detail and nuance help us feel as if we've met these folks and they are now our friends as well. In the honest and moving sharing of her own story, Schwolsky sheds new light on how public health policies, cultural norms, and challenges to old ways of thinking are all part of the fight to save lives and the struggle for a better world."

—Leslie Cagan, lifelong social justice organizer, former national coordinator of United For Peace and Justice (UFPJ), and founder/coordinator of the Cuba Information Project

"Through the stories of patients at the AIDS sanitarium, the author tells the painful story of a hard stage at the beginning of the epidemic in Cuba that reflects the anguish of living with HIV/AIDS in those early years. *Waking in Havana* provides a valuable record of this experience, as well as the evolution of the program to its current form, where all patients live, study, work, and receive medical attention in their respective communities."

—Dr. Jorge Perez Avila, Profesor Consultante Instituto de Medicina Tropical (IPK) and author of *AIDS: Confessions to a Doctor*

"*Waking in Havana: A Memoir of AIDS and Healing in Cuba* provides a personal and timely look at Cuba's HIV/AIDS program. The author was my guide during an unforgettable visit to this beautiful island at the beginning of the pediatric HIV epidemic. The exchange she writes about so vividly is a powerful example of the cooperation and learning that is such an important part of the global fight to prevent HIV/AIDS and provide the best possible care to those who are living with this disease."

—James M. Oleske, MD, MPH, Director, Division of Pediatric Allergy, Immunology and Infectious Diseases, Rutgers-New Jersey Medical School

WAKING
IN HAVANA

WAKING IN HAVANA

A MEMOIR OF AIDS AND HEALING IN CUBA

ELENA SCHWOLSKY

SHE WRITES PRESS

Published November 2019
Printed in the United States of America
Print ISBN: 978-1-63152-654-1
E-ISBN: 978-1-63152-655-8
Library of Congress Control Number: 2019906675

For information, address:
She Writes Press
1569 Solano Ave #546
Berkeley, CA 94707

She Writes Press is a division of SparkPoint Studio, LLC.

In loving memory of Clarence and Maria Julia
Always in my heart

CONTENTS

The events and dialogue in this narrative reflect my best recollection and sometimes reconstruction of the moments they capture.

The names of the Cubans living with HIV/AIDS and close Cuban friends have been changed to respect their privacy. Professionals, friends and family members who appear in the story are referred to by their real names.

PREFACE

In 1972 I left my two-year-old son with his father at a rural hippie commune north of San Francisco and traveled to Cuba to wield a machete in solidarity with the young Cuban revolution. I was twenty-five years old, restless, idealistic, and naïve enough to believe that leaving my toddler for three months was no big deal.

It was illegal to travel to Cuba then for most Americans. This island, just ninety miles off our shore, was declared forbidden territory by a US government decree in 1962, and has more or less remained so to this day. But I was thrilled to discover a beautiful, struggling country in the midst of a profound social transformation—a brave attempt to create a society based on collective well-being rather than individual gain. Cuba was full of energy and people solving problems together, and I immersed myself in the experience—living and working with other young people from around the world—in a way that changed me forever.

After Cuba my life took many twists and turns—through motherhood, divorce, a nursing career, a decade spent in the trenches of the AIDS epidemic, and, eventually, the pain of becoming a young widow. After each life transition, Cuba beckoned—a place where I could reinvent myself and where, no matter if it had been one year or ten, my Cuban friends and colleagues would welcome me with open arms.

In January of 1996, I celebrated my fiftieth birthday in Havana surrounded by the second family I had found there, who made me a "cake" out of rice with pimientos and olives spelling out my name across the top (a big sacrifice given the food shortages) and sang "Happy Baby Jou-jou," their attempt at an English version of the birthday song. This marked the start of a long-planned six-month stay in Cuba. I had taken a leave of absence from my job as a pediatric nurse in Newark, New Jersey, and would be working at the AIDS sanatorium on the outskirts of Havana, Los Cocos, named for the large coconut palms that dotted the grounds.

What a maze of bureaucracy I had waded through on both sides of the Florida straits to get to this special day! This trip had to be "legal," so I'd applied for a license from the US Treasury Department, which arrived only two days before my scheduled departure. On the Cuban side, I needed permission from the Ministry of Health to work as a volunteer with the Grupo de Prevención SIDA (AIDS Prevention Group) at the sanatorium. I had verbal assurances that this would be fine, but nothing yet in writing.

But there were other hurdles to jump as well—emotional ones that could not be resolved by paperwork and licenses. My husband Clarence died of AIDS in 1990, and I had spent the better part of a decade working as a nurse in a pediatric AIDS clinic. A few years earlier, I'd made a conscious decision to transfer to a different job, which moved me away from the world that had shaped my life for so long. Now I would be spending each day with Cubans who were living with the virus and who—because of the US embargo, in effect since 1962, which kept needed medication from reaching them—were often without adequate treatment. They might get sick. They might die. And although my Spanish was fluent, I wondered if I would be equal to the task of navigating the complex political and cultural divides I would encounter.

Many of my colleagues in AIDS and public health circles in

the US questioned my decision to work in Cuba's controversial AIDS program. Cuba faced widespread global condemnation for its policy of requiring people diagnosed with HIV to live in residential sanatoriums. The program was not without its defenders, who pointed to the low rate in infection on the island as a model for the developing world, and dismissed all criticism. I felt caught between these opposing outlooks, but I was determined to keep an open mind. I would be a sponge—soaking up the Cuban experience and trying to understand it in its own context. By the end of the six months, I had four or five notebooks crammed with observations and a shoebox full of tapes of recorded conversations and interviews.

This book was born from those notebooks and tapes, and from a desire to share the stories that were entrusted to me by the Cubans I came to know at the sanatorium. At first I intended to transcribe the interviews and write them up exactly as they had been told to me. But gradually, as I sat at my kitchen table, pressed "play" and listened to the voices of Hermes, Caridad, Alejandro, Roberto, and others whom you will come to know in these pages, I realized that it was my story too, filtered and shaped by my own unique experience as a survivor of the epidemic in a far different place.

Since my first trip to Cuba in 1972, I have visited the island dozens of times. Now, in 2019, I am still connected to the people I met at Los Cocos. We continue to share the memory of friends lost, the difficulties of finding effective prevention strategies for a resurgent epidemic, and the ongoing discovery of common experience.

Epidemics are usually measured in large numbers—in thousands or in hundreds of thousands infected, ill, and dying. The full measure of the global AIDS epidemic has not yet been taken, and the toll of those infected and affected is already in the millions. But the story of AIDS is also recorded in each individual life that has been changed forever by this microscopic virus. This book opens a window into a few of those individual lives. It is a story of border crossings, unlikely connections, and common ground. But above all, it is a story of healing, love, and remembering.

I celebrated my 50ᵗʰ birthday in Havana, surrounded by my Cuban "family" with a cake made from rice and mayonnaise.

CHAPTER ONE

VENCEREMOS

The sounds of "La Internacional," at full static-y volume on the camp's loudspeakers, awakened us every morning at six. *Arriba los pobres del mundo. De pie los esclavos sin pan.* Arise you prisoners of starvation. Arise you wretched of the earth. We were neither prisoners nor wretched, but who could ignore this stirring anthem to the international working class? I scrambled down from my top bunk and stumbled to the large communal bathroom. Metal beds squeaked, the doors of our wooden lockers scraped across the floor, and toothbrushes clinked against dented aluminum cups as dozens of young women rushed to get ready for a hard day's work. In the men's dorm the same process had begun. As the stirring chords of the "Internacional" faded away, we were treated to another musical selection—Tom Jones, apparently a favorite of Cuban revolutionaries. I laughed each morning as the voice of the singer who seduced women to throw their panties at the stage wafted over our camp in rural Cuba. "My my my Delilah, why why why Delilah" might be followed by "Sugar, da da da da da, Honey Honey da da da da da, you are my candy girl"—well, that at least made some sense on this island of sugar cane. To this day I can't hear Tom Jones without thinking of Cuba.

After a breakfast of *café con leche* and crusty bread, and before

1

the sun had come up over the pineapple fields that surrounded our camp, we clambered into the backs of the trucks that would carry us to our work site, holding bandanas over our mouths to keep out the dust. *"Cuba, que linda es Cuba,"* we sang, *"Quien la defiende la quiere mas."* How beautiful is Cuba. Those who defend her love her more. And then we lifted our fists in a salute to the revolution. *Venceremos!* We will win.

"Good morning, beautiful. Need a hand?" Larry reached a wiry arm over the side of the truck to hoist me in one morning, a wide smile lighting up his dark face. Larry, Ken, and I had joined the Fifth Contingent of the Venceremos Brigade together, recruited from our GI coffeehouse project collective, The Home Front, in Colorado Springs. Miguel, Alex, and Angie—three young Chicano students from the university—rounded out our Colorado contingent. They were the only people I really knew in this group of 140 Americans, and we tended to stick together.

The Home Front was housed in a ramshackle Victorian house with a wraparound porch on the outskirts of town. Colorado Springs was home to Fort Carson, a large army base and the place where many GIs landed when they returned from Vietnam with just a few months left to go before discharge—"short-timers" they were called. Our coffeehouse was part of a network of similar projects at bases around the country that had been started in the early 1970s to create a link between GIs whose experience in Vietnam had turned them against the war and the larger antiwar movement. We were committed to bridging the gap between the mostly working-class drafted soldiers, who weren't always sure of their welcome in the antiwar marches and rallies, and the mostly middle- and upper-class student movement.

The Home Front provided a safe and comfortable space to hang out—watch a film, talk to a lawyer, participate in a discussion about the war, and sit down for a delicious family-style meal. We put out a weekly newsletter, mimeographed on an old machine in the basement. Ken, a freckle-faced country boy from Kentucky who looked too young to have been to war, drove our dilapidated van, the "Blue Bomb," to the base every payday to distribute *Aboveground*, and we heard stories about GIs folding copies into paper airplanes and flying them over the stockade walls to prisoners. Larry, a black GI from Alabama, had done his Vietnam tour and then been discharged with "bad paper"—an other-than-honorable discharge. Over 200,000 Vietnam vets had received bad paper after serving in combat, for minor infractions like being absent without leave or getting into a fight. This type of discharge would follow them the rest of their lives and could affect employment and the benefits they were entitled to. Larry stayed on at The Home Front after being separated from the army and served as our assistant chef and resident stand-up comedian. And then there was me. I had ended up at the project almost by accident, traveling there from San Francisco shortly after my divorce, with my small son, Jonah, in tow, to visit an old college roommate for Thanksgiving, and then staying on to become part of the civilian staff.

When a couple of recruiters from the Venceremos Brigade came calling—they wanted representatives of the GI movement on the trip—I leapt at the chance to travel and see a place where the revolutionary ideas I was just beginning to explore were being put into practice. The Venceremos Brigade had been started in 1969 by student activists from Students for a Democratic Society (SDS) who were looking for a way to show solidarity with the ten-year-old Cuban revolution. They worked out a plan with the Cuban government to bring groups of young people, not as tourists but as workers, to assist the struggling nation to reach its ambitious goal of harvesting ten million tons of sugarcane. By 1971, when I first learned about it, the brigade had already sponsored four trips to Cuba with over a thousand participants.

For me this trip represented a break from a life and a role I was having trouble settling into. I dropped out of college just a couple of years after I started, married right after my twenty-first birthday, had a kid at twenty-three. Two years later I was a single mom trying to figure out how to support and care for my young son and grow into my own mature womanhood at the same time. While many of my friends had already graduated from college and were heading on to grad school or careers—or flinging themselves into the "movement" full-time—I was working part-time as an aide in a daycare center and receiving welfare and food stamps. Living in the collective at The Home Front definitely provided some support—my housemates loved Jonah. Larry carried him around on his broad shoulders as he prepared delicious gumbo, cornbread, and peach cobbler for our nightly meals, and Ken let him sit up front like a big boy for rides in the Blue Bomb. But at night, when I went to my room and tucked Jonah into his cozy bed in the large closet we had converted to his sleep space, I was alone with this small boy who depended on me for everything. Cuba—the Venceremos Brigade—was a chance to step away from all that responsibility and try out a different version of myself for a couple of months. This would be my very own adventure—or "venture" as Jonah called it. He waved good-bye at the airport in San Francisco, holding tight to his father with one hand. In the other he clutched a small Cuban flag. "Bye, Mommy," he shouted, just like the stick-figure little boy in the picture book I had made him to explain my absence. "Have fun in Cuba. Have fun on your 'venture!" It was not till much later that I understood just how long two months was in the life of a young child.

Because it was illegal for us to travel to Cuba in 1972, our brigade boarded flights in Mexico City and we were forced to walk a gauntlet of FBI and Mexican intelligence agents, who snapped our pictures as we made our way to the Cubana Airlines Russian turboprop plane that would carry us to the island. It was only the second time I had used the blue passport tucked into a fanny pack around my waist.

I unzipped the pack and felt to be sure it was still there. When we landed at José Martí International Airport a few hours later, the pilot's voice welcomed us to the "first liberated territory of the Americas" and congratulated us for joining the construction brigades that would participate in the important "Year of Building Houses." We were confused. This was in the days before terrorism alerts and high airport security. We had all stashed sharpened machetes in our suitcases. We had been told we would be cutting sugar cane.

From the airport we boarded school buses and traveled to the work camp of wooden dormitories with an open-air mess hall where we settled in for the six-week stay. After a day of orientation and getting to know each other, we were introduced to the work we would be doing. For the next six weeks we bumped along the same rutted dirt road to the construction site where skilled Cuban workers were already setting up for a day's work.

We were divided into small work groups with two Cuban *jefes*, or chiefs, to lead us. Teams of ironworkers, masons, and carpenters guided us as we mixed cement, placed the steel rods that would support the cinderblocks, and trundled heavy wheelbarrows across narrow boards. We soon discovered that the *jefes* of our group, Omar and Andrea, were as ill-equipped as we were for this work. When they were not doing construction work, Omar was a deep-thinking professor of philosophy at the university with a perpetually wrinkled brow, and Andrea was an economist—small, lively, and practical. She kept the atmosphere light when we got cranky from the heat or the inevitable tensions that arose in our young, intense lives.

The goal was for each work group to complete construction on one cinderblock house in the six weeks of work. At the end of each day, we met to assess our progress, sitting around on unfinished walls and gulping cups of sweet fruit punch. By the time we left Cuba, the Venceremos Brigade had built eight houses in what would become Los Naranjos—The Oranges—a new town for Cuban workers. All over the country, similar groups of teachers, accountants, shipping clerks, and factory workers, released from their usual work duties to form construction brigades, were building. Directly participating in this work was one way for Cubans to earn a new home, and housing was scarce.

Each day I headed right for my spot in the shade of a half-built house, where my job awaited. Nothing could be wasted in Cuba, which was why I had been assigned the task of carefully straightening the nails that had been removed from the framing boards of the cinderblock houses we were building. I spent days pounding nails on a rock with a hammer with a small group of women from other work groups who had also been assigned to this task. I was glad that Angie, the young Chicana student from Colorado, was one of them. We shared stories and camp gossip to pass the time, and I got to practice my beginning Spanish with her and the Cubans who were drawn into our conversations.

"*Mira*, David," Angie whispered one day, pointing out her latest crush—a lean, mustached Young Lord from Chicago who wore a black wool beret pushed back on his head on even the hottest days. "He's too old for you," I hissed as David tipped his cap and sauntered away. Angie was twenty-three, only two years younger than me, but somehow my maternal instincts were triggered by her innocence. She was the youngest of a large family from the small town of Fort Lupton and had led a sheltered life up till then. It was under her mother's watchful eye that we had learned to make tamales, which we sold by the dozens on the university campus in Boulder to raise money for our trip. "But he's so cute," she giggled. "And for you—Victor." Angie had been trying to set me up with a Puerto Rican guy from New Jersey, though I knew for a fact he was pining for her. "I know he's chubby, but he's such a sweetheart, and a great dancer."

"Tell me about your life, Elena," Angie said one day when we had run out of gossip. "I've never met anyone like you before. I want to know all about you." Though the name on my birth certificate and passport was Ellen, she and the Cubans we hung out with all the time had given me the nickname "Elena" and it stuck—yet another way that Cuba transformed me!

So between the *clink clink clink* of our hammers on the rocks, I told Angie about the Northern Student Movement, a branch of the Student Nonviolent Coordinating Committee (SNCC) that I had joined in my hometown of Hartford, Connecticut, when I was just sixteen—catching the bus each day after high school to the impoverished North End neighborhood where I learned what it meant to "walk and talk for freedom," climbing the rickety wooden stairs of old tenement buildings to build support for a rent strike, and picketing the local Cadillac dealership that sold all of its cars to black people but would not hire them. I told her about bouncing on the hard seats of a yellow school bus to Washington, DC, for the 1963 March on Washington.

"Did you hear the dream speech?" she asked, and I described listening, with hundreds of thousands, to the soaring words of Martín Luther King, Jr. She laughed when I recounted the story of infiltrating the Ohio State Fair with a group of fellow students during my brief stint in college. We came into the fairgrounds through separate entrances with pieces of a banner folded in each of our backpacks and then reassembled at a predetermined location. Just as President Lyndon Johnson began his speech, we unfurled the banner, which read "Hey, Hey, LBJ! How Many Kids Did You Kill Today?" It was frightening and a bit ironic that we had to rely on the National Guard to get us out of there and keep the crowd from tearing us apart.

Angie had still been living at home with her family when I headed for San Francisco during the Summer of Love in 1967. She was fascinated by my tales of the hippie commune I lived in there—a Victorian house across the street from Dolores Park, painted red, yellow, and blue, where we grew our own vegetables and ran an alternative school—and the women's consciousness-raising group that I joined. After what felt like endless discussion, we had come up with the name "Red Moon Rising" for our group. (We were fans of the local band, Creedence Clearwater Revival, and their song "Bad Moon Rising," which had just been released.) We set ourselves the ambitious goal of organizing young high school women in San Francisco to "join the movement." We passed out flyers at their schools at lunchtime and hung around trying to start up conversations. It was rudimentary organizing and not very effective, but we were just getting started.

As the women's group gradually became more "political"—studying Marx and Lenin and then more current revolutionary leaders like Malcolm X and Amilcar Cabral—I still had one foot firmly planted in the hippie culture that had brought me to San Francisco in the first place. When a group of student and community activists claimed a piece of vacant and long unused land that belonged to the University of California in Berkeley to turn into a People's Park, we crossed the bay with our young students from the alternative school we had started and joined in the work—digging garden beds, planting trees, and building benches and seesaws. And when the university threatened to take back the land and turn it into a parking lot, we took to the streets with our kids and thousands of others in what had been planned as a peaceful protest. I was seven months pregnant and found myself running with a shawl pulled down over my face to protect against the stinging assault of tear gas, herding the kids together, heading away from the confrontation. Angie gasped at this point in the story. "I can't believe you did that," she said. "You must have been so scared. But the baby was okay?"

I put down my hammer and reached a dusty hand into the pocket of my overalls, pulling out the wrinkled picture of Jonah I carried everywhere—and even slipped under my pillow while I slept. His wavy, reddish-brown hair was blowing in the wind, and his chubby legs were planted firmly on a grassy hill in the park. He had hoisted the blue canvas backpack I used to carry him around over one little shoulder—it was as big as he was—and was grinning at his accomplishment.

"Here he is. Totally fine. He's staying with my ex, his dad, in the country near San Francisco."

Jonah's father was living in a trailer on land that belonged to a friend, a rural commune that seemed like a safe, tranquil place for Jonah to stay while I was gone. Steve was glad to have him there. He could run around freely and learn about nature. "I'll take good care of him. Don't worry," he had assured me.

The brigade recruiters had told me the same thing. "There will be other parents on the trip. Don't worry." But I had yet to meet one with a child so young.

Angie, with her pretty smile and sassy demeanor, soon became the center of a group of Puerto Rican and Chicano *brigadistas* and Cubans who hung out together after our workday was done. By default, as her sidekick, I was included and struggled to keep up with their rapid-fire Spanish conversation and understand the jokes that flew around the circle. Most of the Latino brigadistas, I learned, had been avid followers of the Cuban revolution, which for them was an inspiring example of what they wished for their own struggles. Listening to their conversation, I realized how little I really knew about Cuba.

I had been thirteen when the July 26th Movement of workers, students, and peasants had carried Fidel Castro and his *guerrilleros* down from the Sierra Maestra mountains and into the streets of Havana in a triumphant, if unlikely, victory march. The corrupt and oppressive US-backed dictator Fulgencio Batista, who had deposed an elected president in a coup in 1952, had fled in disgrace, and the Cuban revolution was launched. Two years later, I was fifteen when the US again backed the wrong team—a band of over a thousand Cuban exiles in a paramilitary force trained and financed by the

CIA. They invaded Playa Girón on Cuba's southeast coast and were repelled by the fully mobilized Cuban people, led by Fidel himself. The following year, I had just begun to define my own strong political opinions when the Cuban Missile crisis resulted in a thirteen-day standoff between the US and the Soviet Union, which led us all to fear we were on the brink of nuclear war. I received my first D ever on a paper written for Mr. Gale, my favorite social-studies teacher, in which I argued that the US bore equal responsibility for the crisis because of its warlike threats. This was my first experience with the consequences of unpopular political beliefs. The paper was perfectly written; it was my opinion that earned it a D.

Though I had carefully reviewed all the articles in the thick packet the brigade provided before the trip and attended all the study sessions, I still had a lot to learn. In Cuba, I was learning from people who were *living* the revolution—by doing, not reading. After a hard day's work, we often sat up half the night singing and talking, sometimes in marathon meetings to resolve problems that had come up in our community of young people. It had only been ten years since the Cuban government had officially declared Cuba a socialist state. The revolution was still young, and we were making a contribution to it. Our spirits were high, if our carpentry skills were sometimes lacking.

Often we were joined by international brigadistas from Chile, Argentina, Spain, and Mozambique who were staying at a camp not far from ours. I grew close with Andres, a Chilean student who introduced me to a musical group from his country, *Los Angeles Negros*. One of their songs, "Y Volvere" ("I Will Return"), about lovers who have to part but will find each other again, was popular in Cuba and Latin America at the time, and we listened to it over and over again. On September 11, 1973, I watched in horror as the TV news showed scenes of yet another US-backed military coup in Chile that overthrew Salvador Allende, a democratically elected socialist president who was a friend to Cuba, bringing death, torture, and disappearance to thousands. Andres and his fellow students had been so full of hope. I wondered what had happened to him, to them, as I listened in my own safe home to the strains of his favorite song.

Political debates were passionate. My youthful experience in the civil rights movement and antiwar organizing, even our study in Red Moon Rising, had not prepared me for these serious discussions of strategy and tactics and the intense disagreements that followed. The Left was growing increasingly splintered in the US, but the fifth Venceremos Brigade threw people together from the Black Panther Party and the Young Lords, La Raza Unida, Students for a Democratic Society (SDS) and its more radical Weathermen split off, women's consciousness-raising groups, Vietnam veterans and antiwar activists, more old-school organizations like the Communist Party, and some of the young Marxist-Leninist formations of the New Left, along with some former gang members and long-haired hippie types. It was a heady and often confusing mix, at which I'm sure our Cuban hosts were sometimes shaking their heads in wonder. We argued fine points of current politics long into the night as if the future of the world depended on our answers: What is the best strategy to end the war? Was the Soviet invasion of Czechoslovakia justified? How can the US working class be organized? Is the black power movement truly revolutionary?

And we waged our own internal brigade struggles as well. There was one job in our construction crews that women were never invited to do. There was only one cement mixer in our region, and it was making the rounds of the many construction sites, so rather than wait for it to arrive, we mixed the cement in wheelbarrows which then had to be wheeled across a narrow plank on an upward incline so that the heavy wet material could be shoveled onto the flat roof in formation. Why can't the women try, we asked? Look how strong some of us are, and how puny and weak some of the men are. Why should it be a gender thing? Whoever is strong enough should have a chance. Period. We got our wish and then took turns struggling to move this heavy, unwieldy, wheeled instrument of torture up the plank until all but a few of us had collapsed in failure. Unfortunately, I was not one of the triumphant women and returned to my spot in the shade to straighten more nails. But we had made our point—success depended on physical strength, not gender.

Once we debated all night to decide the fate of a brigadista who had been accused of sexual assault. He was a former gang member from the streets of Chicago, and she was a hippie from California. His excuse: she was dressed suggestively and flirting with him, and he was drunk. After much agonizing discussion guided by our Cuban mentors in the spirit of "criticism–self criticism" that was new to most of us, we (including the young victim of the assault) decided to give him a choice. He could spend a few weeks in a Cuban reeducation camp and rejoin us at the end, or he could go home immediately. He chose the camp, did his time there, and was accepted back by all, including the young woman he assaulted, for our two-week trip around the island. The Cubans, however, drew the line at allowing him to climb Pico Turquino, the highest peak in the Sierra Maestra, the region from which Fidel and his *guerrilleros* had staged their revolution. This climb was considered an honor, to be conducted only by invitation. The Cubans took the idea of personal transformation seriously, and we were getting an education in how it was done.

On Saturday nights we drank *guachipupa*, a delicious and deceptively strong rum punch, and danced salsa to the sounds of a local Cuban orchestra. I finally followed Angie's advice to check out Victor, a broad-shouldered *Nuyorican* with a big, soft body and a mischievous smile, and we started spending a lot of time together. He was the best dancer in the camp and in constant demand on the dance floor. He even made me look good as he led me through a pattern of complex moves and twirled me around. After the parties, Victor and I walked and talked for hours. And on Sundays, our only day off, we strolled through the nearby town, where we bought cones of creamy Coppelia ice cream. Victor watched in amusement as I tried out my Spanish on the locals.

Victor told me about his family in Puerto Rico and listened to my stories about my son, Jonah, and my worries about how he was doing without me. There was no way to be in touch with family in the US, and I had not had any news of him since we'd said good-bye at the airport. I had begun to really question the choice I had made, waking early in my bunk to thoughts of my curly-haired little boy clutching his bedraggled stuffed lamb to his chest, curled up in his bed at his father's trailer in the country with one fist under his cheek. I imagined him asking his dad every morning when he awoke, "When will I see Mommy? Will Mommy be home today?" How could I have left him like that, so soon after my separation from his father, which already had been a major upheaval in his tender young life? I had made him a picture book to explain my absence, and we had read it so many times its pages were wrinkled and worn, ripped in places. How could I have thought that would be enough?

Victor hugged me close and reassured me. "He'll be fine, *mi amor.* You'll be with him again in no time." Victor understood what it was like to be without a mother—his own mother had left him and his older sister when he was just eight to be raised by their father after the violence and abuse in their marriage had become more than she could bear. She had been afraid to take them with her but visited their school playground during the day to sneak time with them. He told me about the time she brought him a new shirt as a gift and handed it over the chain-link fence. When he got home that day with the shirt on, his father knew immediately where it had come from and beat him until he was bruised and sore. After that, he kept his mother's visits secret.

There was a depth of honesty and sadness underneath Victor's jovial exterior that was drawing me in. We were falling in love with

Cuba and with each other. Some nights we stole away to the pineapple fields and made love in the dark moist soil between the spiny plants.

When our house-building work was finished, the whole brigade went on a two-week tour of the island, driving hundreds of miles in hot, crowded school buses. We sometimes pulled over along the road in the countryside for what the Cubans called a "pee-pee, ka-ka" stop. I'm sure the sight of a couple hundred young Americans, all wearing bright orange T-shirts with the Venceremos Brigade logo emblazoned on the front, running through the cane fields looking for a private bathroom spot made quite an impression on our rural Cuban friends.

We visited daycare centers, schools, hospitals, sugar cane factories, and neighborhood meetings of the CDR (Committees for Defense of the Revolution). Everywhere we went, we were greeted by children wearing the red-and-white uniforms of the *Pioneros* youth group. They sang revolutionary songs and recited poems by José Martí, the father of the Cuban nation, with a confidence that startled us. The revolution was young. The energy and spirit was infectious. Whatever problems and challenges there were, we were sure that the Cubans would overcome them.

As my time in Cuba drew to an end, I began to prepare myself for going home. We made our return trip on a converted Cuban cattle boat to St. John's, Newfoundland, in Canada, where stormy seas off the coast of the Carolinas confined all but the hardiest in the group to our bunks. Several months after we got back, James Eastland, a conservative Southern congressman, would stand up on the floor of Congress and read all of our names into the Congressional Record, calling us, in rather colorful language, "missiles in human form which have been fashioned on that communist island and fired at America." We certainly didn't feel like missiles as we huddled together on that cold, rolling boat.

I was anxious to see my son, but I didn't know what else would await me. I had quit my job in a daycare center in Colorado Springs, and I learned from brigade leaders that the Home Front GI organizing project had disbanded while I was away. Victor wanted me to join him in Hoboken, but I didn't feel ready.

I headed to California for a reunion with Jonah, who seemed to have grown at least a foot while I was away. And he was talking in sentences! "Dog bite," he said, pointing to an angry purple scar that bisected his left eyebrow. Steve told me the story. A dog that hung around the ranch had taken a chunk out of his forehead and Jonah had been rushed to the nearest hospital for emergency surgery. At one point they had been worried he would lose his eye. There had been no way for Steve to contact me in Cuba. I was horrified. The fact that I had been absent during this traumatic event in the life of my young son reinforced the guilt I was already feeling about having left him for so long. But there was nothing I could do about that now.

Jonah and I moved to Denver, to a small wooden house with a cement stoop in a working-class Mexican neighborhood that we shared with two roommates. I got a job in a silkscreen factory with fantasies of reproducing the silk-screened posters of Che Guevara I had seen in Cuba, but instead I learned to wield a long rubber squeegee to create banners that read "Special Sale . . . Canned Peas . . . Two for $1.00."

A few months after our return, Victor joined me in Colorado when we were stunned by the news that our dear brigadista friend Angie had been tragically killed in a car accident. It was only when we attended her wake and funeral in her hometown that we learned her full name—Angelica Cecilia—and were surprised to see our beloved *compañera*, whom we were accustomed to seeing in denim overalls with a bandana tied around her long thick hair, lying in her satin-lined coffin in the white gown she would have worn at her wedding.

Before the year was out, after many long-distance phone

conversations and lonely nights, I decided to make the move to New Jersey. Jonah and I traveled from Denver on a Greyhound bus with all of our worldly possessions in two suitcases, a big one for me and a small one with Jonah's things that he could barely drag behind him. "Lambie," his little gray lamb with its matted fur and torn seams, made the trip with us.

Victor was a leader of the New Jersey branch of the Puerto Rican Socialist Party (PSP), and it often seemed like he was the unofficial mayor of Hoboken, the mile-square densely populated city that we now called home. When we went out for a walk on the wide main avenue, Victor greeted and was greeted in turn by everyone he met. On Saturdays, he sold *Claridad,* the PSP newspaper, on the streets. We spent most Sunday afternoons sitting on the plastic-covered, red velvet couches in his mother's living room in the South Bronx, and I watched closely to try to learn the secret of her *arroz con pollo*—prepared in her tiny kitchen in a dented aluminum pot that always seemed to produce just enough flavorful rice and chicken, no matter how many people dropped by.

Victor became a warm and loving stepfather to Jonah, and though we never married, we forged a strong family. A year after I joined him in Hoboken, we had a baby girl and named her Angelica in memory of the dear friend from the brigade who had introduced us. Victor loved telling the story of her birth—how he almost delivered her himself with an inexperienced nurse, because the doctor was nowhere to be found. And he loved carrying her high on his shoulders as he walked through the streets of his beloved community.

But the melancholy I had noticed in Cuba beneath Victor's jovial demeanor was deepening. Though he filled his days with political activity and commitments, his nights were often spent drinking and brooding. He had trouble holding a job, and his party comrades began to distance themselves. He was still the loving and gentle "Papi" to the kids, and the life of any party—but after the party was over, he became unreliable, prone to fits of anger, depressed. He lost friendships, political connections, and jobs while I watched, feeling helpless and, increasingly, like I needed to get out of this relationship to save myself. We both tried our best to hold our family together. Cuba and the experience we had shared there was a strong bond, but not strong enough to overcome the challenges of our many differences, the weight of the trauma that Victor was carrying, and his inability to confront his alcoholism. We separated after seven years, but worked to remain friends. Victor continued to drink too much for too many years and died much too young.

Victor and I had always dreamed of returning to Cuba, the island that brought us together. Sadly, that would never happen for him. But I kept on dreaming. The new ideas and inspiration I had taken from my experience in Cuba wove through all the ups and downs of my life. For me, Cuba was a place of warmth, light, and hope. I knew I would return. I just didn't know how—or when.

Angelica, my daughter's namesake, in the back of a truck heading to our worksite.

CHAPTER TWO

FORBIDDEN ISLAND

A midst a pile of unpaid bills and junk mail on the Formica table in my kitchen, where it had sat for a couple of weeks, a colorful brochure caught my eye: "REALITY TOUR TO CUBA, JANUARY 1991."

I had shifted the pile around to eat my solitary breakfasts and dinners during the week, but it was Saturday, and I needed to tackle the bills. I pulled the brochure from the pile and curled up with it in the recliner in the corner of the wood-paneled room that served as my living room. We had moved our bed downstairs to make it easier for my husband, Clarence, to get to the bathroom, and I hadn't yet had the energy to move it back and shift the furniture around, though the hospital equipment that had taken up much of the space in the light-filled front room was long gone. Going back to work and trying to get through a day without crying had taken all the energy I could muster. Murphy, our neurotic mutt, whined at my feet and brushed her tail across the worn carpet, begging for her morning walk. "Murphy, go lie down. Good girl. Go lie down," I said, pointing to the dog bed in the corner. When my life had been an endless stream of caregiving tasks, I had looked forward to escaping into Murphy's walks, but now I found her attention-getting behavior annoying. I just wanted to go through my mail in peace.

I still thought of the recliner as "Clarence's chair," where he used to sit to count out and organize his pills every Sunday afternoon, with a football game on in the background. I put my feet up, rested on the worn spot in the nubby fabric that had once cushioned his head, and read the brochure from cover to cover.

Global Exchange was sponsoring the trip around Christmastime. I quickly did the math in my head. January would be eight months since Clarence died. The trip was for health workers and teachers to learn about Cuba's advances in medicine and education. Ten days. *Celebrate New Year's Eve in Cuba!* the text invited, alongside a photo of colorful folkloric dancers. The thought was enticing, but also scary. I could escape all of the holiday festivities that would only make me feel more alone. I could celebrate my forty-fifth birthday in Cuba. The structure of the trip appealed to me, but the enforced togetherness felt daunting. I was still not quite myself in groups, fragile and shy.

Several days passed before I got up the courage to call the San Francisco number on the brochure. "You've got to come," said the enthusiastic young woman on the other end, after she had answered all of my questions. "You'll love it!"

I had been yearning to make a change in my life, to do something that would turn me away from the cycle of illness and mourning that had occupied the three years since Clarence had been diagnosed with AIDS. I was a young widow. My kids no longer lived at home. Could this trip be the start of something new?

When Clarence first got sick at the beginning of 1988, I had looked for an easier job and accepted a nurse case-manager position at a pediatric AIDS clinic in Newark. Working in a clinic would be good, I had thought at the time—nine to five and not too demanding. I'd spent two years as a union organizer for nurses in New York City and no longer wanted a river separating me from Clarence or a union leader exhorting me to work harder and longer. A lot of my friends thought I was crazy. "You're nuts," they said. "Are you a martyr? You'll be living with AIDS twenty-four-seven." But I was drawn to the commitment of the staff, the sense of mission. Clarence had been forced onto the frontlines of this epidemic, and I wanted to be there too.

But after several years, I was tired and wrung out—"burnt up," as the mother of one of my young patients once named what she saw in my face. "You must be so burnt up," she'd said sympathetically when I couldn't keep my tears from flowing at the sight of her sick little girl during a home visit. I spent most of my evenings in the recliner watching mindless TV or poring through old photo albums, searching for memories to hang on to.

In my work with families facing the great calamity of AIDS, I was often struck by the clarity with which they could recite the day, month, and even minute that their lives changed. When I sat alone in Clarence's chair at the end of the day, I found myself replaying those events in my own life . . . the "before" in the picture . . . as if somehow, by rewinding the tape, I could change the outcome. My story always began with that first drive to the hospital.

It was still blustery and cold in March of 1988, which came in like a lion that year and then never really went out for me, because time stood still for a while. Clarence was shivering in the seat beside me while I navigated the shortcut through the Meadowlands to get to the hospital faster. I drove the route automatically, as I would a hundred times in the months to follow. We approached the outskirts of Jersey City through marshy swampland dotted with old brick factories, passing the Bulk Mail Center where Clarence had worked for more than a decade. We had met in front of that building during a wildcat strike—introduced by our dear friend Tami who was matchmaking on the picket line—and had been living together for eight years.

Our relationship was stormy with a few breakups along the way, but we had held it together. Clarence was forty, an African American Vietnam Veteran who had been struggling to put his life together since the war, with a young daughter from a marriage that hadn't lasted long. I was a bit older, twice divorced with a son and daughter. Our shared political activism and love for music helped, along with the connection to our kids. And the ripple of sexual attraction, the "chemistry" that had been there from the start, stayed strong through all our ups and downs. The early years were the hardest; these were marked by Clarence's heroin use and his efforts to stop—a cycle of remorse and reconciliation that was repeated many times before he finally entered a twelve-step program and found a way that worked for him. It had been five years since he'd picked up a drug or a drink. We had relaxed into an easier life.

By the time we reached the emergency room entrance, Clarence seemed too weak to walk from the car, so I ran and got an aide with a wheelchair to bring him in. The front desk clerk looked up from her papers and gave me a long look. "Are you his social worker?" she asked. I was dazed from the drive and confused by her question. Then it dawned on me that, in 1988, a white woman bringing a sick black man to the hospital must be some kind of professional, his social worker, his nurse.

"No, I'm his wife," I said, though it wasn't really true, not yet. His wife, partner, lover? How many times in the years that Clarence and I had been together had I needed to explain our relationship? I was furious. I didn't need to be dealing with this right now, in an emergency.

Clarence had been bothered by a nagging cough for a month and had been to the doctor a couple of times. He had even stopped smoking, but the cough persisted. I was worried it might be something more serious. By then I had taken care of a few kids with AIDS and seen this kind of cough before. But I hesitated to voice my fears. He's been clean five years, I reassured myself. "Denial is not just a river in Egypt," Clarence had often said, commenting on addict behavior in recovery. Despite what I knew, I was clinging to denial. If I didn't say it out loud, it wouldn't be true.

We sat in the ER waiting room for a long time, but no one came to check on Clarence. Finally an aide arrived with a thermometer. A hundred and five degrees. Suddenly everyone was moving fast. We were in an examining room, and Clarence was on the hard, cold table. Still we waited hours for test results and a room. The hospital insisted on a double isolation room, and there were none available. I dozed in a straight-backed metal chair in the small cubicle, while Clarence slept and woke, and shifts came and went. Time was melting, and the world outside the ER was falling away. A resident came in, pulling the curtain behind him, and Clarence's sickness was given a long name—Pneumocystis cariini pneumonia. Oh yes, I knew what PCP was. I'd seen it many times in my work as a nurse. And I was also aware that young healthy men didn't get this rare lung disease unless their immune systems were severely damaged. *But he's been clean for five years,* I thought, trying to shift the direction this was going in my mind. *How could he get the virus after five years?* It must be a mistake. It couldn't be. But I knew better.

Clarence was finally moved to a real bed in the ER, but there was still no isolation room available for him. I tried to get some sleep on a hard recliner in the family waiting room, kicking off my shoes and wrapping myself tightly in a shredded cotton blanket. After a few minutes spent breathing in the stale smell of too many all-night vigils, I returned to Clarence's bedside. Friends came in the middle of the night to bring me coffee I didn't drink and food I couldn't eat. I stepped outside the automatic doors of the ER to get some air, but I wouldn't go any farther. During all that time, no one touched Clarence but me. Gloved hands placed the thermometer in his mouth and were quickly withdrawn. Food trays were left to grow cold outside the cubicle. I bathed him, placed cool compresses on his forehead when his fever rose, held his hand, watching and waiting.

By the time we were moved to the Intensive Care Unit, Clarence's breath was coming in shallow gulps. Everyone sprang into action, and I had to wait outside. When they finally let me come back in, Clarence was hooked up to a respirator and a heart monitor and all kinds of other tubes. Liver failure, they told me, and kidney failure. But he's strong, and young, they said—he has a chance. A chance? By this time the sickness had another, shorter name. Clarence had AIDS. The word finally spoken out loud landed with a thud in a hollow place in my chest and took my breath away.

We spent days in the ICU, and life moved slowly back to "normal." A TV was wheeled into the room. The canned laughter of sitcoms and the drone of network news competed with the *hiss-thump-hiss* of the respirator. Friends visited. Clarence couldn't speak because of the tube in his throat, so we gave him a clipboard to write short messages. I waited anxiously the first time he asked for a pen, afraid he would write: *Take me off this machine, I want to die.* Or hoping he would write: *I love you, Elena,* which would have been somewhat uncharacteristic, but I thought maybe this experience might have changed him. *Jesse? Chicago?* he scrawled, wanting to know if Jesse Jackson had won the Illinois presidential primary the night before. Clarence was back.

One by one, tubes were disconnected and machines moved away. The respirator was the last to go. When they finally took out the breathing tube, Clarence gagged and then managed a weak smile and a thumbs-up sign. I let out my own breath in one long sigh. I too was finally coming up for air.

Clarence was still weak, walking with a cane when we brought him home, but without the daily trips to the hospital, my life began to seem almost normal. I returned to work at the clinic full time. We moved our bed down to the living room because the stairs were too hard for Clarence. My daughter, Angelica, a sophomore in high school, had to adjust to all of this—she spent a lot of time out of the house and never invited any friends over. My son, Jonah, went back to college, and Clarence's daughter, Kiwan, visited on weekends.

But the disease had moved in with us. It was ever-present. In the corner at night, when I was awakened by Clarence's tossing and turning, AIDS was sitting on its haunches like a feral cat whose eyes glinted yellow in the darkness. It roamed the house in the day, lazily settling into sunny corners, almost tame. I sensed it had the power to pounce unexpectedly and leave long red claw marks on my skin. I was always on guard. We had crossed an invisible line into a zone from which we would never fully return.

At the clinic I was part of a team—me, a social worker, an attending doctor, and a caseload of about seventy-five families. On our clinic day, we saw kid after kid, spending hours drawing blood and starting IVs in an airless exam room. We made home visits to help families learn about their child's illness and treatment and visited schools and daycare centers to educate the staff. All day long we answered phone calls from frightened family members. *She's had a bad rash since yesterday. He keeps on coughing that same dry cough all night long.*

When it was my turn to be on call for a month, I carried a beeper. The beeping alarm almost always meant a crisis, usually that a child had taken a turn for the worse, often that a child was dying. Kids went downhill fast as we ran out of ways to treat them. In the late 1980s, AZT was the only treatment available for most people. It worked well for a while and then stopped working at all.

At home each night, I marked the slightest changes in Clarence's condition, looking for new symptoms. Was that soft, dry cough that woke me in the night the start of PCP pneumonia again? Could the itchiness that caused him to scratch at his arms and legs be an early sign of kidney failure? Was the numbness and burning in his legs a side effect of his medication, or evidence that the virus was advancing in its destruction of his body? When I asked Clarence about any of these symptoms, he brushed off my worry. As his strength slowly returned, he spent his days in a whirl of activities—Narcotics Anonymous meetings, antiwar veterans protests, demonstrations against apartheid in South Africa. He was *living* his life. What was I doing with mine, besides going to work and worrying about him?

The winter of 1989 at the clinic was a tough one. It seemed like my team went to at least one funeral a week. We found humor where we could, laughing together at the way Aisha, one of our first and now oldest patients, called her disease "full-grown AIDS." We were like a M*A*S*H unit, cracking jokes and working like crazy to keep from feeling the losses. Even the terrible sight of one father's attempt to open one of the locked hospital windows and hurl himself out, upon learning that there was nothing more we could do for his daughter, was met with suppressed laughter at the drama he had created.

I turned down invitations to the movies, to dinner. My friends were worried, sometimes annoyed. I listened to their problems and frustrations with only half an ear. The recitation of their petty ups and downs sounded like the static between stations on the radio. Only AIDS came through clearly to me then.

On February 11, 1990, Clarence and I sat together for hours and watched the television, spellbound, as Nelson Mandela was released from prison in South Africa. We had been out since early morning tying yellow, black, and green ribbons—the colors of the flag of the African National Congress (ANC)—to every tree and telephone pole in town so people would know that something important was happening. Clarence squeezed my hand as the dignified warrior walked slowly and proudly to freedom. "Don't you understand, babe?" he said. "If Nelson Mandela can survive twenty-seven years in the racist South African jails, I can lick this thing—I know I can." I too was inspired by Mandela's courage and perseverance. I wanted to believe that Clarence's determination to live was enough. But his was a different kind of life sentence, and he was in a different kind of jail.

It had been two years since Clarence's diagnosis. The medications weren't working anymore, and he was losing weight. I called his mom for his favorite recipes, cooked him pork chops and mashed potatoes smothered in gravy. He would take a bite or two and then put down his fork, apologizing and passing his plate over to me. I gained a pound for every one he lost. "Don't worry about it, honey," his mother told me. "You need the cushioning now."

Clarence just kept getting thinner and weaker. I wanted him to join a research study and try the experimental treatments I read about every day in the clinic, but he refused to spend any more time with doctors.

A soundtrack of worry played constantly in my mind. I was afraid Clarence was losing his battle but couldn't bring myself to say the words aloud. He was trying so hard to stay positive and hopeful. My unspoken thoughts thickened the air between us. *I don't want you to go back to the hospital. We could get a hospital bed. You should stay here with us, with your family.* The doctor offered one final option, a special intravenous form of nutrition that might help Clarence. It was a long shot, he said, and there was risk of infection. Clarence would have to be admitted for a surgical procedure to implant a port for the IV, but he was willing. "You never know, babe. This might help me turn the corner," he said. So we got ready to go back to the hospital.

A lot had changed in the two years since we'd first walked through the doors of this small Catholic hospital. No more double isolation rooms, no more gowns and masks just to take his temperature. I was treated with compassion. Clarence, so frail and old looking with his stick-like legs and arms, charmed the nurses with his toothy smile and self-deprecating humor. An army of friends vied for the chance to visit day and night.

The doctor had a serious conversation with us. Clarence was not doing well, and we had to make some decisions. His mother and I talked it through together. We knew what he wanted—no aggressive treatment, no resuscitation, no respirators. Not this time. Yes, we were sure. We signed papers and prepared for the worst.

I spent all day and most nights at the hospital, just sitting by Clarence's bed, stroking his arm. We had brief conversations. "I love you, babe," he said, more times than he had probably said it in all the ten years we had been together. He was sweet, concerned for me. *Don't sit too long. Eat a little something. Get some rest, babe.*

I had returned home from the hospital to sleep for a few hours when the call came. I glanced at the clock and saw it was five in the morning. It couldn't be good news.

"Your husband is not breathing well," the nurse said. "He's not conscious at this time. We need to know if you want us to do anything more if he stops breathing."

She was waiting for my answer, but I couldn't make any words come out of my mouth. My skin was cold, clammy. I was shaking. "I'll call you right back," was all I could manage.

I called Clarence's mother, needing to share the terrible weight that was bearing down on me. "Mommie, Clarence isn't breathing too well. They want to . . . I know . . . Yes, yes, I'll call them back . . ."

I drove on automatic pilot over roads I knew by heart. I wanted to feel his warm, bony arm over mine. I wanted to feel the whisper of his breath on my cheek.

Please let me get there in time.

Please, please wait.

When I approached his bed, Clarence's eyes were closed. His chest heaved with every breath. Sometimes there was such a long pause that I leaned over to be sure that he was still breathing. The nurses disconnected the monitors and the IV. After a couple of hours they stopped checking his blood pressure. Friends and family gathered in the waiting room.

Every once in a while Clarence shrugged his shoulders and raised his eyebrows as if to say, *I'm doing the best I can, babe.* A couple of times I was sure I felt an answering squeeze to my grip on his hand. He never spoke or opened his eyes. Someone went to get Kiwan at school, and finally she was at his bedside. "I'm here, Daddy. I'm right here beside you." Would she ever really know how much he loved her, how important she was in his life?

A breath or two later and he was gone.

We had made so many sacrifices for this disease. We shopped for AIDS and cooked for AIDS. We scrubbed the house for AIDS. We spent Sunday evenings counting out pills and tablets and capsules for AIDS. We made love wrapped in latex for AIDS. We bought the portable TV and the new mattress for AIDS. And then we bought the commode, the cane, the shower chair, and the walker—all for AIDS. We would gladly have sacrificed more—we would have sold the car, we would have moved to a first-floor apartment, we would have bought the hospital bed and the IV pole . . . we would have done anything that AIDS required of us . . . but finally there was nothing more to do. Clarence's struggle was over. The hospital-supply companies came and got their stuff. I was left behind.

I gave over the funeral plans to Clarence's family, insisting on only a couple of things. "I don't want any of your corny folk music at my funeral," he had said one night, looking up from his book. "Make sure you have *my* music." We enlisted a local quartet to play Coltrane's arrangement of "My Favorite Things." At the funeral, friends got up and spoke about Clarence, about his impact on their lives. They told funny stories, but I didn't really hear them. Their words were distorted and wavy, as if they were carried to me through thick green water. There was an expanding peacefulness inside me . . . and an aching, *aching* loneliness.

Though I was not an observant Jew, I liked the custom of acknowledging the mourning period by bringing people together, sitting *shiva,* so I opened the house to friends for a few evenings. The dining room table was always full of food. One acquaintance, not a favorite of Clarence's, brought a rhubarb pie with a whole-wheat crust. It was half-cooked and bitter—a health-food pie—and no one ate it. Clarence would have gotten a kick out of that, I thought. For months I would see or hear something and think, *Clarence would have liked that, Clarence would have hated that, I wonder what Clarence would have thought about that.*

It had been six months since Clarence died, but I was still asking myself what would Clarence have thought, what would Clarence have done, as I struggled with the decision about whether to sign up for the Cuba trip. I had stayed so close to home during his illness, as if drawing an invisible circle around our lives would keep us safe. But not Clarence—he had traveled to Panama with a veterans' peace delegation in November of 1989, just six months before his death. I remembered how thin and frail he looked in the video footage of the trip, but so happy—a wide grin breaking across his gaunt face. I was anxious the whole time he was gone—about parasites and food and whether he would remember to take his medications. Then I realized the trip was Clarence's way of saying, "Don't count me out. I'm still here." I could almost hear his gravelly voice now in my head: *Go for it, babe. Go to Cuba. Why not? You'll learn stuff and meet interesting people. You'll have a good time.*

The adventure of travel was appealing. I had always loved the feeling of reinventing myself in a new and totally different environment. Even though it was not my first trip to Cuba, it had been twenty years since I'd been there. I was sure a lot had changed. *I* had changed.

One more doubt surfaced as I imagined myself in Cuba again. I had read articles about Cuba's policy of quarantine for people with

HIV/AIDS—requiring people who are HIV positive to live in special institutions. The AIDS community that I was part of had been severely critical of this policy. The headline of a story in the *LA Times* about a delegation that visited one of these sanatoriums trumpeted disapproval: "Cuba's AIDS Quarantine Called Frightening." If Clarence and I had lived in Cuba, he would have been forced to enter a sanatorium, and I would not have been allowed to go with him because I was not infected. We would have been separated by the virus. How could I visit a country that would have done that to him, to us? But it was a country I loved. I wanted to see and understand for myself, through my own eyes and experience. I would visit the AIDS sanatorium, I decided. I would talk to people living with HIV/AIDS and hear their stories. I'd talk to nurses and doctors. I remembered Cuba as a place filled with warmth and compassion. I would keep an open mind.

I seesawed back and forth between going and not going for a few more days and finally called to make my reservation. *Why not?* I told myself. *What have you got to lose?* The group would meet in Cancun on December 27th and leave for Cuba the next day.

The night before the trip, with my bag packed and waiting by the door, I relaxed in the recliner and looked through the old photo album again, pausing at a family portrait that had been taken just months before Clarence died. I laughed when I remembered how hard the Sears photographer had worked to balance the skin tones of Clarence and his daughter, Kiwan, with my daughter Angelica's olive-tinged complexion, and the pinkish hues of my son, Jonah, and me so that we would all look natural in the photo. A blended family indeed! I had wanted that picture so badly—to capture the whole family together before it was too late. Clarence had his usual big grin on his face, but I could see the telltale signs of illness—the weariness in his eyes, the way the blue and purple tweed jacket hung loosely on his thin frame, the bluish tinge to his lips. My hair was shorter, dyed auburn, and I was trying to hide my plump body under a loose-fitting ivory dress with large red roses scattered across it. My smile looked pasted on, and my gaze was far away.

An old yellowed Polaroid was tucked into the binding at the back of the album. As I gently dislodged it, I spied myself—laughing and singing in the back of a truck, my arms around my comrades, dressed in denim overalls, my hair tied in a red bandanna. Suddenly I sensed beside me the spirit of that laughing girl, and I reached out to embrace her fearlessness. *I am going back to Cuba!*

Clarence and me, healthy and happy, in the time before AIDS.

CHAPTER THREE

REALITY TOUR

No FBI agents were snapping photos when we left the Cancun airport for Havana on December 28, 1991, even though we were violating the travel ban, but I was more nervous than I'd been the first time I took this trip. So much had happened in my life and in the world. I was no longer the idealistic and naïve young woman I'd been twenty years ago, and Cuba might not be the same young country I remembered, so full of revolutionary energy.

Our group of about thirty—nurses, social workers and teachers—buzzed with excitement as we boarded a Russian-made plane that looked like it could have been the same one that carried me to the brigade twenty years earlier. This time I didn't have a machete in my suitcase, just some pamphlets from my pediatric AIDS program, pencils for the kids, and barrettes, lotion, and other small gifts I planned to share with Cubans I met along the way. And this time, I had no guilt about leaving my kids behind. My son, Jonah, was finishing up his last year at Bard College and my daughter, Angelica, was a senior in high school. I was confident that she could take care of herself while I was away. I thought fleetingly of her father, Victor, and that I was returning to the place where we had met. Our relationship had ended badly, and though I was grateful that he had attended Clarence's funeral, he had a new family and we rarely spoke.

The night before our departure for Cuba, the Global Exchange tour leaders brought the group together in the lobby of our modest hotel in downtown Cancun, far from the tourist resorts on the beach. We got to know one another over guacamole and margaritas. Ana and I hit it off immediately. She was a teacher about my age from LA—a short, thick-bodied Chicana with coppery skin and lots of shiny black hair pulled up in a bun—and I was drawn to her spirit of adventure and irreverent humor. Soon I was cracking jokes, laughing easily, sharing what I knew about Cuba with the group. Already I felt lighter.

The written trip itinerary was jam-packed with activity—visits to hospitals, schools, Cuba's much admired family nurse-doctor program, the Center for Sex Education. We would be busy. The fact that Ana and I both spoke fluent Spanish would come in handy. "Just keep in mind," our tour leader cautioned us, "we have to be flexible in Cuba. Our schedule may change when we get there."

And change it did. Our Cubana jetliner plunked us down smack dab in the middle of the "Special Period in a Time of Peace," or *Periodo Especial*, that had been newly declared by the government—trying to put a positive spin on the severe economic crisis brought about by the collapse of the Soviet Union, Cuba's main trading partner. Cuba had lost its favored-nation trading status with the Soviet bloc, and with it 90 percent of its fuel and close to 85 percent of its export market. Over two hundred new goods were added to the rationing system that had been in place since the revolution. Foods that had been abundant on the shelves of government markets became scarce. Tomatoes, potatoes, cooking oil—even black beans, a staple of the Cuban diet—became impossible to find.

To make matters worse, the US Congress chose that moment to expand the embargo—making it harder for Cuba to obtain needed supplies from other countries. The embargo, or *bloqueo* (blockade) as the Cubans called it, had been in place since 1960, when it was imposed by President Eisenhower after Cuba nationalized US oil refineries. It prohibited the US government and corporations from trading with Cuba, but under new regulations, third countries whose ships docked at Cuban ports would also be penalized by being kept away from US ports for a period of six months. The noose around Cuba's fragile economic stability was being tightened.

I was also aware that this could have dire consequences for Cubans with HIV/AIDS. American pharmaceutical companies made all of the medications in the AIDS cocktails that prolonged life in the US. Under the rules of the embargo, they were not allowed to sell these lifesaving medications to Cuba.

No announcement welcomed us to the "first liberated territory of the Americas" this time around. Instead we began our "reality" tour of a small country struggling to stay alive. Hospitals were sending home all but the sickest patients. Schools and universities were closed. Many workers had been furloughed. Fuel shortages were creating waits of up to three hours at every bus stop, and *apagones* or power outages occurred every day, sometimes lasting for hours. Hotels were mostly not affected because they had their own generators, but half of our scheduled visits had to be scrapped.

Our Global Exchange guides and Cuban liaison scrambled to find suitable substitutes for visits that had been cancelled due to the crisis. It soon became clear that we'd have a lot more free time than had been planned.

Ana had friends she'd met on a previous trip. One night we visited Raulito, a young curly-haired English teacher sporting a Guns 'n Roses T-shirt, in his family's small apartment in a dark, damp building in central Havana. Raulito's father regaled us with stories of his pre-revolution work as a waiter at a café in Havana where Che

Guevara and Camilo Cienfuegos, two heroes of the Cuban revolution, used to come to eat (and perhaps to plot, I wondered). María Luisa, Raulito's neighbor, a young actress who was hugely pregnant and on bed rest, invited me to keep her company in the cramped sleeping loft built above her kitchen where she was spending her days. I clambered up to lie on the bed next to her, and we talked for hours, like long-lost sisters sharing giggles about Raulito and Ana's growing flirtation, and all the dreams María Luisa had for her unborn baby. She was one of the first Cubans I met who seemed to be truly interested in hearing about my life. I discovered a kindred spirit who would become a friend for life.

One night Raulito came to see us at our hotel overlooking the *Malecón*, Havana's romantic sea walk where couples and families strolled at night. He brought a fellow teacher, a tall, lanky, and very serious young man named Alfonso. After we polished off a bottle of Havana Club, Alfonso kissed me. He was much younger than I was, and I would probably never see him again, but I tried not to think about that too much as I lost myself in the startling pleasure of being caressed. Once again, it seemed, I had found a bit of romance in Cuba.

There were other nurses who did AIDS work in our group, several from New York and San Francisco. We traded stories from our time in the trenches, sharing the weariness and instant camaraderie we'd all developed as witnesses to the ravages caused by this epidemic. Now that we had some unscheduled time in the trip, we approached our guide to request a visit to the AIDS sanatorium on the outskirts of Havana. We had all heard the same negative comments about how Cuba was treating people with AIDS—including forced indefinite quarantine in a sanatorium for all HIV-positive people regardless of health status. Cuba defended this isolation policy as a necessary public health measure to prevent a widespread epidemic, and claimed to be providing state-of-the-art care. I found it hard to believe that the Cuba I loved so much would imprison AIDS patients and treat them harshly. I was apprehensive but didn't want to miss this opportunity to see and judge for myself.

While our tour guide worked on getting permission for the visit to the sanatorium, we were invited to a meeting at the home of an American journalist who had been writing articles about Cuba's AIDS program. Karen had lived in Cuba for many years. Her house, in a quiet suburban neighborhood, was small but comfortable and boasted several of the visible marks of foreign privilege in Cuba—a relatively new stereo and TV, and a number of well-fed, healthy-looking cats and dogs roaming about. By contrast, most Cubans were desperately trying to maintain twenty-year-old Russian appliances, and their pets had to struggle for their daily ration like everyone else.

We gathered in the air-conditioned living room to escape the heat—a group of about fifteen, sitting in a circle in chairs and across the tiled floor—and began our introductions. Some of us were health-care professionals—doctors, nurses, social workers. Some had lost best friends, lovers, or husbands to AIDS. Several in the group were Cubans living with HIV/AIDS who had received permission to join us.

As the discussion moved slowly around the room, we had to strain to understand one another. Language was not the only barrier—cultural and political differences also colored our perceptions. Javier, a Cuban family physician, explained how Cuba's policy developed out of the fear of an out-of-control epidemic like that in Africa and in the United States.

"In the beginning we didn't know much about the disease, and it was very frightening," he told us. Cuba stopped importing blood and began to screen all blood donors. That's how Javier had discovered that he was HIV positive. Now he lived in the sanatorium and worked as a doctor in the clinic there.

Javier was a handsome man in his early twenties with pale skin, dark wavy hair, and a lively speaking style. "We thought at that time that we could isolate people there until a vaccine or a cure was found." He spoke emphatically and gestured broadly as if delivering a talk at a lectern. "We hoped we could prevent a devastating epidemic. And it is working. Just look at our numbers."

Alexei, a soft-spoken, slightly built older man spoke next, his voice gathering strength as he described his experience. "That first year in the sanatorium was very hard," he began. Alexei was an artist and used to a solitary lifestyle, working and living alone. "Being with all those different people was uncomfortable, and I felt very closed in," he went on. "Now things are not so difficult. I can get permission to leave when I need to—like to come here today." For Alexei, there were certain benefits to living in the sanatorium. He didn't have to stand on a ration line for food or compete for scarce consumer goods. We were surprised to hear him describe his air-conditioned apartment in the sanatorium, since we had been imagining a hospital-type setting. He was comfortable there. But, Alexei admitted quietly, if he could, he would probably choose to leave.

A nurse who worked at San Francisco General Hospital, in the epicenter of the American AIDS epidemic, described conditions there. She spoke of crowded emergency rooms where people sometimes waited days for a bed in the hospital, of the fear of rejection and discrimination that haunted her patients, of those she had seen die alone and afraid. She wondered aloud how many of her patients, if given the choice, would trade their "freedom" for the community and security found in Cuba's sanatoriums.

As stories were shared, my mind raced. I kept circling back to Clarence, trying to picture him spending the last years of his life in a restricted institution, unable to travel or dedicate himself to the political activism that had kept him going. *Cuba is different*, I told myself. *Don't try to compare. Just listen.* But I felt stuck in my own head, struggling to absorb the conversation around me.

Then it was my turn to speak. My voice shook as I struggled with conflicting emotions. I began by describing the children and families that I worked with in Newark. When I mentioned the numbers of infected children—two hundred in our clinic alone—the Cubans gasped. There were only four or five known pediatric cases in Cuba, due to a policy of routine screening for HIV in the first trimester of pregnancy—something that had yet to be implemented in the States. Most HIV-positive Cuban women, under societal and peer pressure and with no legal obstacles, opted for abortion rather than take the risk of bearing an infected child. I described the multiple losses faced by families—and the daily struggle to survive, to provide shelter, food, and clothing. I listed all of the obstacles they faced in seeking medical treatment and care.

Finally, I talked about Clarence and his two-year battle with AIDS. "The last years we shared together were so important to both of us," I said, looking around the room and gathering the courage to speak my mind. "As a person who is not HIV-infected, according to the official policy in Cuba," I went on, "I would have been separated from him—not allowed to live with him in the sanatorium. How can you justify separating families in this way?" My voice sounded too loud in my ears, but I plowed ahead to finish my thoughts. "I don't understand it. I can't accept it." The room was quiet, and I felt raw and exposed.

Orlando broke through the uncomfortable silence and responded to me in a firm voice. A robust auto mechanic in his early forties, Orlando had been infected while serving as a civilian with the Cuban army in Angola. He returned to Cuba and, unwittingly, transmitted the virus to his wife. They had a young son who was hanging out in Karen's yard waiting for his dad to finish the meeting. He would answer my question, Orlando said, but first he wanted to tell me a few things about the sanatorium, and about people with AIDS in Cuba. He had heard that people with AIDS in the US are from groups that had been discriminated against even before AIDS came into their lives—gays, African-Americans, Latinos, IV drug users.

"Here in Cuba," Orlando began, and I knew I was about to hear another little speech, but I gave him all of my attention, hoping to understand. "Here in Cuba, most of the people who are infected with the virus are like me. I was serving my country—fighting for freedom in Africa. I regret a lot of things, but not that. I am considered a hero here in Cuba." He went on to describe other respected members of Cuban society who acquired the virus when they were serving as diplomats or artists traveling abroad on official missions. Because Cuba is an island with little tourism, the AIDS virus was brought home by this small group of Cubans who were allowed the privilege of travel. Presumably most were infected through sexual liaisons abroad. I wondered if that was true for Orlando, but he didn't say.

"It's different here. I like my life. I receive the best medical attention. I leave the sanatorium to work every day. I can leave on weekends whenever I want to." We had been told that patients who are judged *confiable*, or trustworthy, by a panel of doctors and psychologists were allowed to leave the sanatorium for short periods. Orlando had provided us with an example of that policy as he continued describing his life. "The government pays my salary even when I am not working and maintains my apartment in Havana. My son goes to a boarding school, and we are all together at home on weekends. If they opened the doors completely tomorrow and said 'go,' I would ask to stay!" Orlando leaned forward and seemed to speak directly to me. Could he hear my thoughts, which were still stuck on the issue of family separation?

"You talk about family," he said. "In Cuba maybe we have a different concept of family. My family includes my neighbors, my doctors; it includes those who share my life in the sanatorium. We are not trying to separate families; we are trying to protect the whole society.

I don't always think only of what is best for me, I think about what is best for my country. I didn't ask to have this virus, but I do. I accept that, and I accept that I have to protect others."

I didn't argue with Orlando. I knew that his ideas were a genuine reflection of the values he was raised with and believed in. I remembered the early years of the epidemic in the US and how no one in government would even say the word "AIDS." At my clinic, we had to deal with the prejudice and stigma that our patients faced every day and the fear that this disease created. Some families drove halfway across the state to get their medications so that there would be no chance that someone in their community would discover their situation. We heard about Ryan White burned out of his home, and kids with AIDS thrown out of school. People with AIDS were left to advocate for themselves, and often fend for themselves—and they fought to protect their rights.

But the protection of individual rights came with a price. I thought again about my own situation. Clarence chose not to get tested and didn't find out he was infected until he was very sick. Since there was no cure or real treatment for the disease and lots of potential for discrimination if he had a positive result and it became known, his decision seemed to make sense. But that put me at risk. What if I had become infected? And even after he was diagnosed, no public health person counseled me about getting tested myself or followed up with me. I waited until he was out of danger to be tested, and three weeks later, after hearing nothing from the doctor, had to call to get my negative results over the phone.

Cuban patients are asked to provide a list of their sexual partners who might be at risk of infection, and they are all contacted and tested. Everyone goes along with this policy because it is no different from the procedure followed for other contagious diseases, and it is for the common good. How many infections could have been prevented by that kind of epidemiological detective work in my community? How many kids might not have died? Could Clarence have been saved if he'd been tested earlier?

I was peeling away layers, trying to understand this epidemic in a context so different from my own—a country where public health is seen as the right of the people and the responsibility of the government. This was AIDS, certainly with pain and individual loss and suffering, but without the dying children.

Orlando spoke forcefully, but he was quick to laugh when we chatted for a few minutes in Karen's yard. He wanted to be sure I really understood what he was trying to express in the meeting. Orlando reminded me a bit of Clarence—his energy and confidence, his selfless dedication to what he believed, and his sweet concern for me. His son, José, a husky ten-year-old who had been waiting patiently for his dad, finally tugged him away, and I rejoined the group for the trip back to our hotel.

Several days later, we received permission for our visit to the sanatorium and boarded a small, air-conditioned tourist van for the forty-minute trip to Santiago de las Vegas, a neighborhood on the outskirts of Havana. The road out of Havana proper was filled with hitchhikers, and every bus stop was crowded with people waiting for whatever might turn up to transport them—private cars, horse-drawn carts, even dump trucks had been called into action to move people around the city.

When we finally turned off for the sanatorium, I was surprised by the tranquil, tree-lined driveway that carried us into the institution. There was a guardhouse and a gate that had to be opened to allow our van to enter, but otherwise it looked far different from the locked-down prisonlike place I had expected to see. Whitewashed buildings were surrounded by flowering bushes and well-manicured lawns. In its former life, the sanatorium had been the estate of a rich Cuban and then served as a rest and recreation center for the Cuban military. It felt like an oasis from the noisy bustle of Havana.

We made our way to the administration building, a colonial-style hacienda with a red-tiled roof and cracked tiled floors, and took our seats on the creaky wooden chairs in the auditorium, where we were greeted by Dr. Jorge Pérez, the director of the sanatorium and architect of Cuba's evolving AIDS program. He was a small, fast-talking man with twinkling green eyes who echoed what Javier had told us at Karen's house, about the need to nip the epidemic in the bud: that Cuba, as a small developing nation, could not afford to care for hundreds of thousands of infected people. I thought of Haiti, where Belinda, one of my favorite patients in Newark, had been born. On that island, AIDS had already become the leading cause of death for sexually active adults, and hospital beds were filled with the sick and dying.

After Dr. Pérez's orientation, we were invited to tour the grounds and talk to some of the residents, who were referred to as "patients," since this was officially considered a hospital. We saw a range of housing—from dormitory-style buildings to small apartment complexes to single homes in the newer section of the sanatorium. Patients, who had clearly been alerted to our visit, stopped to chat with us on the paths and invited us into their homes.

I felt uncomfortable wandering in and out of people's homes, but it was the only way to really get to talk to them, and I wanted to speak with as many patients as possible. César, an artist like Alexei, showed us around his small, bright apartment hung with his colorful abstract acrylic paintings. Sergio showed off his large German shepherd and the framed black-and-white photos he had taken of Cuban musicians and actors that lined the white walls of his apartment. Many of the patients I spoke with seemed genuinely enthusiastic about the care and support they received here and honest about some of the things they didn't like—the constant monitoring of their private lives, the need to get permission to leave on visits to family, and sometimes the requirement to have an *acompañante* (a companion, usually a worker from the sanatorium) with them.

At the end of the tour, we visited a crafts workshop where several patients were busy making mosaic pictures with shells, painted greeting cards, and tiny straw witches that could be hung on the rear-view mirror of a car. I had learned that some patients, like Orlando, left the sanatorium to work each day, while others had jobs within the institution. This "recreational therapy" seemed designed to keep those who had no work busy at something—productivity was an important cultural value in Cuba—and perhaps to bring in a little revenue from visitors. I bought a Cuban *sol*, a sun fashioned out of palm leaves and beans, and hoped that it would make it home in one piece.

As we prepared to leave, I had a chance to speak with a few of the doctors who worked in the sanatorium. Like the people at the meeting in Karen's house, they were shocked by the numbers of children we cared for at my program in Newark and the scope of the epidemic.

One energetic young doctor gave me his card. On the back he had scribbled an address. "I'm Arturo," he told me. "Come and hear me play piano at the Hotel Habana Libre on Friday if you can." I stashed the card away in my bag, curious about the doctor who played piano in a nightclub. Sadly, I wasn't able to take him up on his invitation, as our tour left Havana the next day to visit the countryside.

We spent New Year's Eve in Santa Clara, a small and pleasant provincial capital in the center of the country, at an outdoor party hosted by the local CDR. This organization functions like a combination block association and neighborhood watch—carrying out health campaigns, educating residents about new policies, mobilizing for mosquito control. At the time of our visit, the CDRs also reported on any suspicious goings-on in the neighborhood, like foreign visitors or black market activity, surveillance activity that is no longer encouraged.

After the party, we walked through the balmy night air back to our hotel. Suddenly, on both sides of the streets, windows were thrown open and water came pouring down onto the pavement. We laughed and ducked. I knew that Cubans cleaned their tile floors by sweeping water out the door, but wondered why people were cleaning their houses on New Year's Eve. Later we learned that it is a custom to throw water to clear the house of the bad times of the past year and to welcome the new year with hope. This hope felt fragile in a country at the beginning of a "special period" of economic hardship and uncertainty, but in Santa Clara on January 1, 1991, everyone was celebrating.

The ten days of the tour had gone by quickly. I was glad we had some breathing room to explore on our own, and I had made some good new friends. I had carried Clarence with me on this trip, but I had also walked alone in the world for the first time in a long while. I was anxious to share what I had learned with my colleagues at the clinic. Maybe we could donate some medications, since the embargo extended its tentacles even into the importation of lifesaving drugs. And I was hopeful we could invite some Cuban doctors and nurses to participate in our international training program. I felt alive and full of new ideas. This trip had lifted the weight of the past six months off my shoulders, but now I had to go home. I was anxious about the reality that awaited me.

After the constant companionship of my fellow travelers, my apartment felt empty and silent when I climbed the stairs and opened the door after the all-day trip home. The air was overheated and stale. There was nothing much to eat in the fridge. No one was there to greet my arrival. Angelica had left a note on the kitchen table—she was visiting a friend and had taken our dog, Murphy, with her. I would have one day to rest and recover, and then it would be back to work.

Once the excitement of sharing trip photos and presenting what I learned to the clinic staff wore off, I found it harder and harder to get up each morning and face my day. What did I have to look forward to now? I needed to make a change.

I revisited my old idea of grad school. Public health or social work? I wasn't sure which would be a better path for me, but the public health degree required fewer credits, which became the deciding factor. Finishing up some undergraduate credits, prepping for the Graduate Record Exams, and filling out applications gave me a future to focus on and kept me busy for a year.

When I was accepted at Hunter College in New York City, I made an even bigger change. Tami, the dear friend who had introduced me to Clarence on the picket line more than a decade earlier, offered a couple of cozy rooms in the finished attic of the large Victorian house in our same small New Jersey town, where she lived with her partner, Karen. This would help me save money on rent while I was paying for school, so I packed up and moved. Clarence's chair wouldn't fit up the narrow stairs to the attic, so his mom offered it a home and took our dog, Murphy, along with it. The noisy warmth of my friend's blended family, with several daughters and stepdaughters still at home, enveloped and comforted me. When Angelica came home from college on summer break, we all spent hot, muggy evenings perched on the porch swing, watching fireflies and drinking cold beers. We were one big chaotic bunch.

I was still working at CHAP, the Children's Hospital AIDS Program, while I studied part time. We had started an international training program, and my colleagues were enthusiastic about inviting some Cuban doctors and nurses to participate, and about traveling to visit the island themselves. By the end of 1992, we had begun to build an exchange. Over the next couple of years, I traveled to Cuba several times, both to recruit Cuban participants for the training program and to serve as a guide for groups from CHAP.

Looking for contacts who could help, I found the business card of Dr. Arturo, the doctor who had invited me to hear him play the piano. He became our first "exchange student" from Cuba, and for three months he lived at the house I shared with Tami and her family. Dr. Oleske, the round-faced, large-bellied, white-haired elf of a man who directed the CHAP clinic, nearly caused a riot when he visited the largest children's hospital in Havana. Striding through the wards with his trademark purple bunny in the pocket of his lab coat and a Polaroid camera in his hands, he started snapping pictures of kids and offering them to their mothers. Film was really hard to come by in Cuba due to the economic crisis, so no one had photos of their kids, and soon there was a group of mothers from all over the hospital crowded into the ward we were visiting, each clamoring to have a photo taken and watching in amazement as the picture of her child slowly took shape on the Polaroid film.

During one of my exchange trips to Cuba, María Luisa, whom I had met in 1991, invited me to dinner. We had remained good friends. I had visited shortly after her daughter, Lucía, was born and was proud to be her honorary *titi* or auntie.. Throughout the economically difficult years of the early 1990s, I tried to help María Luisa's family as much as I could, supplying vitamins for Lucía, filling her eyeglass prescription, and bringing support hose for María del Carmen, her grandmother, and makeup for María Luisa, who was an actress on Cuban film and television. Sometimes I slept over in the small apartment she shared with her husband Omar, María del Carmen, and Lucía. There was only one bedroom with two double beds, so when it was time for bed, we all piled in. María Luisa called it "the Cuban pajama party."

María Luisa's cousin Tony was also visiting. A short, handsome man with a large Spanish nose and a wire brush of a mustache, he invited me to take a bike ride around the city the next day. On a bridge over the Rio Almendares, where we stopped to rest, he leaned over my bike and gave me a sweaty kiss. He was an agronomist, an agricultural scientist, recently divorced with a twelve-year-old daughter, and like many divorced people in Cuba, had found himself homeless due to the shortage of housing and Cuba's unique and cumbersome practice of "trading" rather than renting or selling houses. He was couch-surfing at various relatives' homes when I met him.

We saw each other several more times during that trip and then kept in touch by faxed letters and static-y phone calls where our words echoed back at us. Calls were placed through Canada, as there was no direct phone communication between the US and Cuba. Over the next several years, I saw Tony every four or five months, and we rekindled our romance each time. Sometimes he joined me in my hotel, though this was against the rules. In a policy some Cubans called "tourist apartheid," Cubans were not allowed to visit tourists in their rooms or eat in hotel restaurants. The restaurant rule has changed, but unfortunately the "no visiting the room" policy has remained in place. Sometimes we stayed together at María Luisa's. Despite its long-distance frustrations, the relationship grew. We talked about spending more time together—a difficult hurdle to get over for a US-Cuban couple. At a time when many Cubans were emigrating, sometimes with the help of a foreign romantic partner, I had found the one Cuban who was adamant about not ever leaving Cuba. His professional life and his daughter were too important for Tony to leave behind. I was busy with grad school. For the time being we would just have to keep on as we were.

In 1994 I was invited to be a keynote speaker at an International Nursing Congress in Cuba, and I organized a US delegation to attend the conference. I had presented at AIDS conferences in the States, but this would be the first time I would bring my personal experience as the widow of someone who died of AIDS into a talk—and in Spanish no less. I titled the speech "From Both Sides Now: When AIDS Comes Home . . . *De Ambos Lados: Cuando SIDA Llega A Tu Casa.*" It took me days to write, and when I stood to deliver it, facing hundreds of nurses from all over Cuba and Latin America, my knees were shaking and my mouth was dry. Would the audience understand my Spanish and get my message? "*En el año 1988, mi mundo se puso al reves cuando mi esposo fue diagnosticado con SIDA,*" I began, looking down at my notes. My confidence grew as I told some anecdotes from my dual experience as a caregiver to my husband and to hundreds of children with HIV/AIDS. I finished to thunderous applause and a standing ovation.

During the question-and-answer period, a nurse from the Dominican Republic rose to ask me how Clarence had gotten AIDS, something I had deliberately omitted from my talk. I didn't want to label him as a "drug addict" in front of this large audience or to fall into the judgment and blame that had penetrated even the world of professional AIDS caregivers. Before I had a chance to formulate a response, she was shouted down by voices from all over the auditorium. "None of your business. Why are you asking that? What difference does it make how he got it?" I sat down in a daze. After the session, I was thronged by nurses from Panama, Columbia, Nicaragua, and Mexico who embraced me and wished me well.

Many of my classmates in grad school were younger than my children, but I was enjoying the challenge of learning new things and even, for the first time in my life, striving for good grades. I was anxious to finish my degree and see what awaited me, but it was taking forever, and I had a hard time dragging myself to class after a long day at work. When a job opened up in Early Intervention, a program to support developmentally delayed children, I applied for a transfer out of the AIDS clinic. After a decade on the frontlines, I was ready to step back.

My coworkers threw me a huge farewell party, where I prepared myself to be both toasted and roasted. We had a tradition of writing spoofy songs for special occasions and had even created a doo-wop style singing group, AZT and the Side Effects, to deliver them. The humor was a good balance to the sadness and loss that lay underneath so much of our time together. They decked me out in a crown and sash, proclaimed me "Miss Cuba," and topped this look off with a real Cuban cigar. A David Letterman–style "Top 10 Reasons Why Elena is Leaving CHAP" started off with "#10: Lost her beeper," then "#9: Looking for new colleagues to appeal to for contributions to her causes." Reason #1? "Wore out her funeral attire."

At my new job I served as the center nurse in the Early Intervention program, but mostly got to play with the babies and toddlers, and to interact with their moms when they came to group sessions. Some of the kids had severe disabilities—they were blind and deaf, or spastic and unable to move without pain—which was hard to see and work with, but nothing like AIDS. I immediately felt less emotionally wrung out. I even had some down time between groups to study, and was able to speed up my progress toward a degree by taking an extra course each semester.

By the end of 1995, I had almost completed my academic coursework. My grad program also required a fieldwork project, and an idea began to hatch. Could I use my connections in Cuba to arrange to do my fieldwork there? Though by that time I was visiting two or three times a year, this might be the chance I had always wanted to actually *live* in Cuba, to experience everyday reality. And Tony and I could see how it felt to really be together as a couple.

My Cuban colleagues were very receptive. Cuba's AIDS policy had continued to evolve, and it was no longer mandatory for HIV-positive people to enter the sanatorium. Instead they were encouraged to spend a couple of months there to have their health evaluated, learn how to live a healthy life with the disease, and protect others. The *Grupo de Prevención SIDA* or AIDS Prevention Group was the only organization of people living with AIDS in Cuba, and they planned to offer a course at the sanatorium to prepare members of the group to serve as peer educators—conducting prevention classes in their own communities for the first time. I received an official invitation to participate in developing the first session of *Viviendo con VIH/SIDA*, or Living with AIDS. I had taken an important step forward and was thrilled.

In the months that followed, new challenges appeared at every turn. I needed permission from Hunter College to do my fieldwork in Cuba, a leave of absence from my job, and enough money to live on for six months in Havana. But the biggest obstacle was the US ban on travel to Cuba, forbidden territory for most Americans. Thousands got around the ban each year by heading to Cancun or Nassau and just buying a ticket, and I had always found a way, legal or otherwise, to get there. But this stay needed to be "official" in order for me to receive academic credit, so I applied for a special research license two months before my scheduled departure. I waited anxiously for it to arrive, checking the mail each day and wondering what "Plan B" I could come up with if it didn't get to me in time or if my request was denied. I had already bought lots of supplies for the trip, solicited donations of condoms and medications, and packed and repacked my bags.

Finally, the day before my flight, I opened an envelope from the US Treasury Department and pulled out a long, legalistic document with lots of fine print. It was my license to travel to Cuba. In the morning, my daughter helped me pack the back of our Subaru wagon with the large black canvas duffel that held all the donations, a suitcase filled with training supplies, and my own small bag with clothing and personal items. In just a few hours I would be in Nassau, where I would transfer to my flight to Cuba. It would be so nice not to have to deal with the cold weather, I thought, as I watched the snow-covered banks of the New Jersey Turnpike whiz by on the way to the airport. I couldn't believe I would be spending the winter on a tropical island.

I had always dreamed of living in another country on my own, of the chance to immerse myself in daily life and lose the *outsider* status of a tourist. Each leg of this journey would take me closer to that dream. I would be living and working in Cuba for six months.

My excitement was tempered by one small seed of doubt. When I transferred to the Early Intervention program, after Clarence's death and all the years I spent watching kids die, I had taken a giant step away from AIDS. Now I was getting ready to climb into the trenches again, spending each day with a group of HIV-positive people in a Cuban AIDS sanatorium—getting close to them, worrying about their health, wondering if they would grow ill and die. Was it some kind of survivor guilt that had brought me to this place, to this work? Like a magnet, AIDS had pulled me back.

My first view of the AIDS sanatorium in 1991. It felt like a leafy, peaceful oasis from the bustling, chaotic city outside its walls.

CHAPTER FOUR

WAKING IN HAVANA

I had only been in Havana for a few weeks, but day by day my life was beginning to feel more settled. Tony had found a room for us to rent in an apartment in the Vedado section of Havana—on a leafy block that was far from quiet. Most mornings, long after he had left for work, a shrill voice from the street below shook me out of a deep sleep.

"*Cebollas, naranjas.*"

The first time it happened, for a moment I wasn't sure where I was.

"*Naranjas y cebollas.*"

I recognized the voice of a neighbor alerting the residents of my block that a shipment of oranges and onions had arrived at the open-air market on the corner.

I still was not completely used to these early morning sounds in my new neighborhood, or to the sight of Ruki, my hostess and landlady, tiptoeing past my sleepy form on the bed. I opened one eye and she threw me a half-apologetic grin. "*Buenas dias,*" I said, trying out my Spanish voice. Ruki frequently stole into my room in the early morning, opened the shuttered wooden doors and peered out over the small balcony to the dusty street below. This had been her bedroom, and the balcony was still her connection to the world outside the apartment walls. She couldn't give it up, but I didn't mind. This life without boundaries in Cuba reminded me of my commune-living days in the 1960s, and Ruki's shuffling steps past my bed had become part of my morning soundtrack in Havana.

Lack of privacy was only one of many things that took some getting used to as I adjusted to daily life in Cuba. Living and working here, as I would be doing for the next six months, felt far different from spending the week or two that had been my experience over the last five years. I was lucky to have found this comfortable and spacious room with a private bath. It wasn't legal in 1996 to rent to a foreigner, especially an American, but lots of Cuban families were doing it to make ends meet.

I couldn't start my work in the sanatorium until my papers were approved by the Ministry of Health, so I spent my days exploring the neighborhood, doing some research in the library, and decorating my room. I had brought a colorful Indian bedspread and some family photos to make it feel like home. To those I added some bromeliads found in a local open-air market, which Tony helped me hang in the windows. These remarkable plants needed only air to survive, which was good because I had a tendency to neglect my plants at home—left behind for my friends to water. They gave a tropical air to the simply furnished room. Or so I hoped.

When I finally emerged from my room, Ruki would already have begun her daily chores. To make myself useful, I had appointed myself her assistant for the tedious daily job of cleaning the rice. Like all Cubans, Ruki had a ration card which entitled her to purchase certain staple foods at greatly subsidized prices—rice, beans, potatoes, cooking oil, a few hard rolls a day, and whatever protein and fresh vegetables and fruit were available. Every couple of weeks she bought a large cloth sack of rice. Her gangly eighteen-year-old son, Miguel, hauled it up three flights of stairs to the apartment, and each day she scooped out the amount needed for the family meal.

Ruki sat at one end of the large wooden dining table. Every day she wore the same simple cotton housedress and apron. Her graying brown hair was clasped on one side with a barrette that made her look like a schoolgirl, and her legs were encased in the support stockings prescribed by her doctor, which she washed carefully each night before going to bed. Her plastic glasses, mended with tape at one corner, slipped down over her nose as she bent over the rice.

From the kitchen I heard the familiar sound of "Radio Reloj," the aptly named "clock" radio, an all-day news station that announced the time every five minutes, accompanied by a loud and syncopated *tick-tock, tick-tock.* The shutters in the dining room, partially open to let in the cool morning air, filtered the bright sunlight into shimmering waves. The rice was spread out on a worn piece of cheesecloth, and Ruki's fingers, though swollen and knobby, moved quickly through the mounds of white grain to find the small pieces of rock hiding within them. My fingers were clumsy at this unfamiliar task, but together we created a large portion of cleaned rice on one side of the cloth. On the other side, a pile of little stones slowly grew. From time to time, a *sinsonte*, a tiny Cuban songbird, flew in the window and swooped back out with a grain of rice in its beak.

"Que haces hoy, Elena? What will you do today?"

Ruki would briefly look up from her work and flash me a smile. She was normally shy and quiet, but during this morning ritual she often chattered away about her life and asked me lots of questions about mine. I think I was the first American she had ever had a chance to talk to personally. She told me about her years of work in a yogurt factory and the pride she felt in having been promoted to supervisor before she retired a few years earlier. Ruki had been raised in Jaimanitas, a small fishing village on the outskirts of Havana, in a very poor family. She was sympathetic when workers, students, and peasants fought to get rid of the long and bloody dictatorship of Fulgencio Batista, and cheered them on when they rode through the streets to celebrate the triumph of the Cuban revolution in 1959. She still sat in rapt attention when Fidel Castro delivered one of his hours-long speeches on TV.

One gray and drizzly morning as we sat cleaning the rice, I spoke to Ruki about my work in the pediatric AIDS clinic in Newark. I told her about the children I cared for and how helpless I felt when they became sick and died so quickly, so young—about their families, grieving and asking why. I searched for words to describe how little I could do to comfort them, how tired I became during those years. And then I told her about Clarence, my husband, and the shock of learning that he too had AIDS—that this disease had come home to my own family. Ruki's busy hands sank into her lap as I spoke that day, her usual barrage of questions silenced by the weight of my story.

Both Ruki and I were widowed in our forties. She was five or six years older than me, but it sometimes felt like we were separated by a generation of differing experience and expectations. Ruki was amazed that my grown children "allowed" me to live alone in my New Jersey apartment and to travel to foreign lands by myself, and that I had chosen to go back to school at the ripe old age of fifty. Ruki's whole family lived with her in her apartment. She and Miguel shared his small bedroom, and her other son Domingo had recently moved back into the apartment with his new wife and her two children. They all lived together in the third bedroom, which was crammed with beds, dressers, and the kids' toys and schoolbooks.

"*Bueno, me voy.* I'm off," I said, pushing away from the table as Ruki swept the cleaned pile of rice into a pot. She did all of the cooking in the morning in anticipation of the possibility of one of Havana's frequent blackouts in the afternoon. They were sometimes planned to save energy and would be announced hours in advance by a car with a loudspeaker going around the neighborhood, but just as frequently they occurred without warning.

"*A donde vas,* Elena? Where are you going?" Ruki asked with a hint of longing. Because of her arthritis, Ruki rarely went out except to visit the doctor or the market on the corner.

"I'll go to the big farmer's market and see if they have any meat,"

I said, grabbing a net bag to take with me. That brought a smile to Ruki's face. On other trips to the market, I had brought back lettuce and radishes and cucumbers—excited to find the makings of a big salad. But Ruki and Miguel were not impressed. That I would spend my American currency, worth so much more than their pesos, on anything other than *carne* was inexplicable and very disappointing.

Ruki was happily preparing dinner with the meat I had brought back from the market, and I was in our bedroom folding the sheets that we had pulled down from the rooftop clothesline that afternoon when I heard Tony's voice in the kitchen. He had returned early from work. The smell of garlic frying in the small piece of *manteca* I had managed to buy wafted into the room. Tony came and sat beside me on the bed. He was grinning from ear to ear, but his hands were shaking.

"I have big news, exciting news, *noticias importantes.*"

"What? What? Tell me!"

"I've been chosen to work in Mexico, as an expert, on an experimental citrus farm," Tony said, and his words sent my heart plummeting. I tried not to let my disappointment show on my face.

"Wow, that's amazing. When will you leave? When will you be back?"

"I leave in two weeks, Elenita. I have a lot to do to prepare. The contract is for a year. It's such an opportunity. There is nothing for me here but more of the same, but in Mexico . . ." His voice trailed off.

"But what about your daughter?" *The one you said you'd never leave? What about me? About us?* I had been looking forward to more weekends with Tony—tooling around Havana on our bikes, exploring neighborhoods that were new to me, visiting the botanical gardens and the zoo, trips to the beach. We had barely gotten started on the life together I had imagined for months from a distance in New Jersey.

I wanted to scream and kick like a toddler denied her favorite toy. But how selfish was that? I was free to travel all over the world, but

Tony had never left Cuba. Of course he had to go. I swallowed my hurt and pulled him close.

"I'm so happy for you, Tony. *Es increíble.* It's incredible. Congratulations."

Two weeks went by quickly. Tony was working nonstop getting everything in order for his departure. And I was busy too with trips to the Ministry to sign papers and to the library to continue my research into Cuba's AIDS program and policy.

The night before his trip, Ruki and I prepared a farewell dinner—a nice piece of fish I had bought at the farmer's market, black beans and rice, and a sweet flan custard for dessert. My friend María Luisa, who had introduced us, came with her daughter, Lucía. Tony's daughter Aineryk took two buses to get there. Right after Ruki served espresso in small china cups, Tony apologized and withdrew to our room to finish his packing.

We said good-bye at the apartment. This was a government mission, and he was picked up by an official government car for the trip to the airport. I didn't know how we would keep in touch or when we would see each other again. So much for trying out our life as a couple. I couldn't hold back a few tears despite my efforts to be stoic, but Tony didn't even notice. He was already halfway to Mexico in his mind.

Finally, the day after Tony left, I got my own official notice—I could begin work on the following Monday. I went to sleep that night with a list of all that I needed to do to get ready for my first day swirling around in my head: figure out what to wear, figure out how to get there by public transportation, review my notes, practice my Spanish. I slept fitfully and dreamt of Tony, surrounded by fragrant orange trees, standing straight and tall with big black boots on his feet and a machete in his hand. In my dream, I waited for him to turn around and see me, but he never did.

*My landlady Ruki spent every morning cleaning the rice–
separating small pebbles and twigs from the grain.
Some mornings I served as her assistant.*

*Ruki tiptoed through my front bedroom to survey the street
below from my small balcony.*

CHAPTER FIVE

LOS COCOS

I arrived at the AIDS sanatorium in the midst of a tropical downpour. At first, all I was aware of was how wet I was and the squishing sound my sandals made as I walked. My small umbrella was useless. I crossed the dirt road through puddles of mud looking for the entrance. The rain came down harder, sheets of gray water through which I could barely make out a gate and a small booth with someone sitting inside. I approached, feeling that this was the right place, though I couldn't see a sign or an address. The gatekeeper glanced at the soggy documents I passed through the rain-streaked window, made a phone call, and then stepped outside to open the gate for me.

Two rows of royal palms flanked a path leading up to the white, once-grand colonial house that I remembered from my previous visit. I assumed this was the administration building—my destination. The path was hard-packed dirt turning into mud in the rain, and I had to jump several large puddles along the way. Large palm fronds knocked down by the water and wind littered the ground, and the air had a heavy metallic odor. Somewhere in the distance, a cow moaned, and I wondered how close it was. One person hurried by me in a blur, carrying an umbrella that had been turned inside out by the wind. As I approached the building, I could see gray cement leaching through old paint and large cracks in the walls. Broken tiles with bits of bright color still clinging to them lined the portico where I was finally out of the rain and could take a good look at Los Cocos, the AIDS sanatorium on the outskirts of Havana where I would be working for the next six months.

I stood for a few minutes in the middle of the porch. The water dripped off of me in rivulets, forming a puddle at my feet. My glasses fogged up in the humid air, and I took them off to wipe them with my soaking wet shirt tail. My hair was plastered to my head, and the canvas bag where I had stored all my papers was soaked through.

Why didn't I take a cab like María Luisa suggested? I wondered. This is not the way to make a good first impression. However, I hadn't wanted to arrive like a *gringa* in luxury that Cubans couldn't afford. Instead I'd taken a *camello*, a sort of a bus invented in Cuba when the fuel supplies dried up in the early 1990s after the fall of the Soviet Union—two full-size buses with the seats taken out joined by a connector that formed a hump in the middle. The whole contraption was attached to the cab of a heavy-duty diesel truck, which pulled it through the streets. Each camello was able to move hundreds of people at a time, standing up and jammed together, and everyone hated them. In the plaza at Santiago de las Vegas, I had to transfer to a horse-drawn wagon that would take me the rest of the way to the sanatorium. And that was when the sky had opened up.

"Elena?" A young woman approached from one of the rooms that opened onto the porch where I was standing. *"Bienvenida—al fin!"* She kissed my cheeks and took my dripping bag. And then, in heavily accented but clear English, she said "I'm María Antonia. We have been waiting for you. Come, let's sit in my office."

While María Antonia busied herself stashing my wet bag, bringing me a towel to wipe my hair and face, and sending word out to bring *café,* I studied both her and my surroundings. I knew from our correspondence that she was head of the Department of Psychology at the sanatorium and would be my boss. She appeared to be not much older than my daughter, not totally surprising since so many young, well-educated Cubans held responsible positions. But still, she seemed young to be a clinical psychologist and department head.

María Antonia had dark curly hair pulled pack from her face by a simple brown plastic band. She was fair-skinned, with deep blue eyes and freckles scattered across her large Roman nose. In the US, her nose would have been the feature that kept her from being called pretty, but I was sure that in Cuba she had more than her share of admirers. She moved with confidence and spoke in a high, thin voice as if every sentence ended in an exclamation mark! I felt soggy and self-conscious in her presence.

"*Dime, Elena,*" she said, returning with two steaming mugs of café con leche. "How are you liking Cuba so far? Tomorrow we'll start preparing the training course. We are so excited to have you here with us!"

I sat up straighter on the wooden chair, tried to ignore the puddle that had already formed on the worn tile floor beneath me, and met her startling blue eyes.

"*Yo tambien,*" I said. Me too.

Every day after that, I stood and waited for the bus to the sanatorium at the busy corner of 19th and H, just a few blocks from my rented room in the neighborhood of Vedado. Diesel trucks spewed gray smoke as they lumbered by. Chattering groups of school kids in their blue and red uniforms raced around me, and long lines of people formed to wait for a bus or truck that would take them to work. Across the broad avenue, a *camello* pulled up and discharged thirty or forty passengers who walked briskly in every direction. I was grateful that the sanatorium was one of the workplaces that provided a special workers' bus. It made it much easier to get to work each day. As I waited, I absorbed all the sights and sounds of a day just getting started and, as always, the friendly, curious stares that let me know I had been marked as an *extranjera*, or foreigner.

I was still puzzled by life in Havana, trying to understand how things worked here. There were all kinds of protocols and unspoken rules that seemed to govern every aspect of life. It was a little like eating an artichoke—I kept pulling off dark spiny leaves, but each layer yielded to another. I was sure that somewhere underneath the layers, the sweet and tender flesh of the heart waited to be revealed, so I kept pulling. I questioned my friends about everything—why are there so few stores, where do you go shopping, how do you rent an apartment, how do you figure out which bus to take, who makes the rules, what happens when you break them? "Elena, please don't try to figure Cuba out," they told me. "It's impossible. You'll never be able to understand it. Even we don't understand it, and we've lived here our whole lives."

On the bus, I engaged my seatmates in drowsy conversation. Alex, a gray-haired psychologist who spent part of each lunch hour making the rounds of the cafeteria collecting table scraps in a plastic bag for his dog, took a special interest in me. "Why Cuba?" he asked me one morning. "How did you get so interested in Cuba?"

"I first came to Cuba in 1972, with the Venceremos Brigade." Alex was old enough to remember the brigade.

I told him how we had built cement-block houses for workers—a whole new town called Los Naranjos—and then traveled around the island for a few weeks. "I don't know—I just fell in love with Cuba, with the spirit and hope I found here." Alex sighed and rolled his eyes. He had a sister in Miami and a rather cynical view of US-Cuban politics. My enthusiasm for his country was lost on him. But Manolo, a tall, lean maintenance worker with leathery skin and a shock of white hair, who often scowled fiercely at me as I boarded the bus, twisted in his seat to look at me with new interest.

Being "found out" as an American embarrassed me at times, even though most Cubans made a big distinction between the US government and "the American people who are our friends." Living in Havana, I could see for myself the hardships caused by US policy, especially the forty-year-old embargo that barred trade and most humanitarian aid. The 1990s were a particularly tough time in Cuba, and I was beginning to understand what this meant on a daily basis. I was glad to see Manolo's scowl soften a bit as I told Alex more about my time on the Venceremos Brigade.

When we finally turned into the long driveway at the sanatorium, I took a deep breath. It was such a welcome change from the noisy bustle of Havana. Even the air was clean, sweet with the fragrance from the many flowering trees that lined the walkways. I remembered the anxiety and conflict I had felt on my first visit to the sanatorium in 1991, wandering in and out of people's homes and invading their privacy. But now I was working here every day, a part of the life in this unique institution.

"Hola chica, como estas?" My "boss" María Antonia breezed into the office and greeted me with a hug and a kiss. The youthful energy and demeanor of my supervisor still surprised me each day, but she was proving to be a warm and wise coach. My work hours were mostly spent in the small, air-conditioned office of the Psychology Department with María Antonia and Chavela, a health educator. We were designing a three-week program to train members of the *Grupo de Prevención SIDA (GPSIDA)*, Cuba's only non-governmental AIDS advocacy group, most of whom lived in the sanatorium. They would be among the first Cubans with AIDS to conduct community-based prevention sessions. Our preparation for the class was laborious and time-consuming, as we often had to wait for access to the only computer in the department. Some of our lessons we wrote out by hand and copied on an ancient mimeograph machine.

We worked in the whitewashed, red-tiled Administration Building, which was left over from the sanatorium's former life as a rest and relaxation center for the Cuban military. The first Cubans infected with HIV had been soldiers returning from Angola and were considered heroes. After their diagnosis, they were housed here and were soon joined by

HIV-positive diplomats and artists. Among a limited group of Cubans who traveled abroad, they had contracted the virus in their travels. Perhaps the status of those first Cubans with AIDS contributed to the better than average living conditions that were provided in the sanatorium. Not for the first time, I thought about how different the trajectory of the AIDS epidemic had been in the US, with the first wave of infection hitting people from populations already reviled and discriminated against—gay men, Haitian immigrants, and drug addicts.

About ten years earlier, the military center had been converted into Cuba's first sanatorium and was now one of eleven throughout the country. It was a large community with a few hundred residents; small apartment complexes and single-family houses were scattered along tree-lined paths. Spending a day here was like hanging out on a pleasant college campus. I was aware that it was not quite the "real world" and that there were many rules and restrictions governing residents' lives, but it was a community in its own right with some very seductive charms.

Chavela, the health educator, plopped down on the chair next to me, picked up the nearest pile of mimeographed sheets, and began to fan herself energetically. *"Hola, compañeras.* Sorry I'm late. The bus never came and I had to hitch a ride." She greeted us with my favorite Cuban word—"compañera." Hard to translate, this word that peppered everyday conversation suggested a more meaningful relationship than *amiga* or friend, and a less formal relationship than comrade. An all-purpose word that could also be used to describe a partner, lover, girlfriend, or boyfriend, compañera somehow wrapped up the warmth and spirit I found in Cuba in a one-word package.

Chavela was short and plump with a mischievous smile, and I had already learned much from her creative approach to health education. The Cuban doctors tended to deliver dry lectures (much like their counterparts in the US), but Chavela spiced her classes with playful activities and games. I enjoyed watching her facilitate an icebreaker and tease a group of serious scientific "experts" into forming animal pairs and joining in a fantasy animal wedding set to music.

It was my turn to lead the class, and the topic was "Safe Sex." I had taught a lot of classes like this in the States to all kinds of audiences, but this time I would teach in Spanish in Cuba. I was nervous. I had spent hours the night before writing out my notes and instructions in Spanish on colored index cards. I still wasn't sure how I would demonstrate correct use of a condom without my customary banana. "Bananas are for eating!" one of my young colleagues had exclaimed, laughing when I asked her if I could obtain one for my class demonstration. Maybe a cucumber? I suggested. Nope. Not that either.

As my students gathered for class in the workers' cafeteria, I gazed around the circle at the small group I had grown so close to in these few weeks: Caridad, one of the founders of GPSIDA, who had lived in the sanatorium since it was created in 1986 and waged a quiet but persistent battle to win dignity for AIDS patients; Hermes, a radio announcer before he was diagnosed, who was the only one in the group who had managed to avoid living in the sanatorium; Tanya, the punk rocker and poet with her platinum blond spiky hairdo; Alejandro, the young computer whiz who had left the sanatorium to live with his boyfriend in the master bedroom of his mother's apartment. There were others who came and went, but this was the core group. They had shared bits and pieces of their stories with me over the weeks we had been working together.

In our conversations so far, I had revealed just the mere outline of my own experience, but it was enough to create a powerful connection between us. They had learned about Clarence and knew that I had worked as a pediatric AIDS nurse for ten years. My "resume" on the frontlines of this epidemic was impressive, though I was very aware of the one credential I did not share with this group—I had been spared infection with HIV. I was not "positive," but "negative"— an irony of language that has always given me pause.

The class went better than expected. My Spanish proved mostly adequate to the task, and Chavela jumped in when I stumbled. We ended with a condom demonstration that dissolved into raucous pandemonium as each member of the group took a turn unrolling a condom on his or her fingers.

"I'll put the chairs back," I offered at the end of class, as Chavela and María Antonia rushed off to make some phone calls before lunch, and I was alone for the first time. It was a relief to stop translating for a while and let my thoughts drift. Then Caridad approached, breaking through my reverie. "Amiga," she said in her quiet voice. "Can you come have a *cafécito* with me tomorrow? We can do the interview you had asked me about." I was planning to interview some of the group members as part of my fieldwork project, and Caridad had been one of the first to volunteer. "Si, *seguro*. Yes, sure," I replied. "That would be great." I had felt drawn to Caridad from the first day we met and welcomed the chance to get to know her better.

Sharing around the circle in our classroom at the sanatorium.

CHAPTER SIX

TIES SEALED IN LOSS

"Did you know that I actually met your husband, Orlando, in 1991 at a meeting?" I was walking with Caridad on the path from the Administration Building to her home. Caridad's house was in a section of the sanatorium known as Marañon, which got its name from one of the many types of fruit trees that spread their leafy branches and provided shade and tranquility. In mango season, the ground would be littered with burnt orange globes. That day, in early spring, the mangos sat green and unreachable on high branches above our heads.

"I'm not surprised you met Orlando," she said as we walked through the tunnel that separated her neighborhood from the rest of the community. "He was so outgoing, so friendly. He knew everybody." Caridad greeted a nurse hurrying to the clinic, a group playing dominoes on an overturned wooden box in front of their small apartment complex, and a man walking his large German shepherd that panted uncomfortably in the hot Cuban sun. She had lived here since 1986, and she too, it seemed, knew everybody.

We stopped to say hello to Norma, who sat alone on a shaded porch in a large cane rocker and acknowledged our approach with a small nod. She didn't rise to greet us. Caridad spoke quietly with her for a moment. Norma was gaunt and frail looking. Her hair was thin and straight and stripped of its natural color, her skin dry and almost translucent, and her eyes dark-rimmed and huge in her shrinking face. I had seen that look many times. *She won't live much longer,* I thought, as we walked away.

"One of the hardest things about living here," Caridad said, as if reading my thoughts, "is watching good friends become sick and die. It reminds you constantly of what you are living with. There is no denial or escape like there would be on the outside."

As Caridad and I approached her home that spring day, only the slap of dominoes on wood and the shout of a triumphant player disturbed the midafternoon quiet in Los Cocos.

Caridad's small white cement and tile house was set back from the path and surrounded by mango trees. It had been built as part of the expansion of the institution for its new use as an AIDS sanatorium. She and Orlando had moved into the house in 1988, a reward for their good behavior and seniority, and for her it was a welcome refuge from the dormitory-style living of her early years in the sanatorium.

Inside, the house was sparsely furnished with several polished wooden chairs and a glass-topped coffee table. It was immaculate. The tile floors gleamed and the whitewashed walls were sparkling. The most conspicuous object, sitting on a lace doily in the center of the table, was a large ceramic doll, ornately dressed in red-and-black lace.

Glancing around the room, I noticed the absence of photos on the walls or table. There were no photos of Orlando or José, their son. None of the family together. Caridad told me she had packed them all away after Orlando's death just eight months earlier. She couldn't look at them. I was struck by how differently each of us processes and moves through grief. In the months after Clarence's death I surrounded myself with photos—framed on the wall, stacks of albums always at the ready next to the recliner in the small living room we had shared. I thumbed through them intently, seeking to bring back every small detail of our life together—to remember his touch, his smell, his voice. Caridad had put everything away, out of sight.

While Caridad busied herself making coffee, I set up my digital tape recorder in the center of the round wooden kitchen table. Part of my field work project would involve taped interviews with Cubans living with HIV/AIDS and some of the professionals I was working with, which I would later write up to document my work.

"Orlando really made an impression on me, even though I only met him once," I said as Caridad set our coffee cups and a small bowl of sugar on the table. I remembered a robust, vital man—brown-skinned and muscular with curly hair and beautiful green eyes. A bit of a flirt, but with a straightforward and simple way of expressing himself.

"Orlando was *unico*, an extraordinary person," she said and settled into her chair. "Not a day goes by that I don't think about him. Everything in this house reminds me of him." I gazed across the table at my new friend. Caridad, or Cari as she invited me to call her, was a small woman. Her wavy auburn hair was cut short and framed a light brown face that was pensive, even severe in repose. Her white blouse had a demure ruffle at the neck, and her jeans were crisply ironed with a straight, sharply defined crease down the front of each leg. She was what the Cubans call *una persona seria,* a serious person. Though her warm smile was easily coaxed from beneath her solemn demeanor, Cari rarely participated in the constant boisterous banter that was so typical whenever a group of Cubans got together.

I pushed the RECORD button, and Cari cleared her throat nervously. "Why don't you start by telling me about the time just before you moved in to the sanatorium?" I prompted, and Cari began.

In 1986, Caridad, Orlando, and their ten-year-old son, José, lived in a small apartment on the top floor of an old building in central Havana. She worked as a secretary in the office of *Granma*, the paper

of the Cuban Communist Party which was published six times a week
and was one of two main newspapers on the island. By then she and
Orlando had been married for eleven years. Her parents still lived
in a small town in the province of Camagüey, several hours away by
bus, but were frequent visitors in her Havana home, often staying for
a month or two so her father could receive medical treatment. Several
brothers and sisters also lived in the capital.

Orlando had been working as an auto mechanic when he volunteered for service with the Cuban army in Angola in 1984. He spent
almost two years there, returning home in 1986. Like all Cubans
returning from a mission abroad, Orlando had to spend a couple of
days in the army hospital for a routine physical evaluation. Then he
could return to his home.

"We planned a big celebration," Cari told me, gathering up the
coffee cups and bringing them to the sink. "There were parades and
parties. They were heroes."

While Cari washed the dishes, I thought about how different
Orlando's experience was from the stories that Clarence had told me
about his own return from the Vietnam War. By the time Clarence
was kicked out of the military with a general discharge in 1971, the
war had become unpopular and spawned a huge antiwar movement.
GIs returned one by one when their thirteen-month tour was over,
and there were no programs to help them with reentry. Clarence had
felt alienated, unappreciated, and completely at loose ends. "I kept
thinking what the hell am I supposed to do now? Just get a job?" he
said during one of our few conversations about that time in his life.
He described being angry all the time, getting into fights, and using
drugs to self-medicate, continuing a habit begun in Vietnam.

He had told me a story about running into a girl he had known in
high school at a record store, where he was browsing through all the
music he had missed in 'Nam. "Vietnam. Wow," she had said. "Did
you kill anyone?"

He had exploded in her face, yelled, lifted a hand to slap her, and then strode angrily out of the store. "I was a mess," he said.

Caridad had returned to the table. She folded her arms in her lap.

"Was Orlando proud to have served in Angola?" I asked. "Were you proud of him?"

I knew some of the history of Cuba's involvement in Angola's civil war, which had begun in 1975 when the first Cuban advisors were sent to help the newly independent Angolan government fend off attacks by rebel forces that were being supported by the apartheid regime in South Africa. Cuba had strong ties to Angola going back to the days of the African slave trade. Men, women, and children were forced from the Portuguese colony of Angola to work the coffee and sugar plantations in Cuba, which was under Spanish control. Many Afro-Cubans traced their ancestry to this part of the continent and felt a strong bond with their Angolan brothers and sisters.

Cuba's operation in Angola had lasted twelve years and became yet another brick in the solid wall of hostility between the United States and Cuba. The US called Fidel Castro an international outlaw and branded his deployment of troops to fight in Africa a "flagrant act of aggression." The Cubans, on the other hand, saw their involvement as an expression of international solidarity. In 1986, the year of Orlando's return from Africa, Fidel visited the troops in Angola and spoke passionately of their efforts to ". . . ensure the revolution and independence in Angola . . . the defeat of fascism, and the elimination of apartheid."

By 1988, the year a peace agreement was finally signed at the United Nations, more than three hundred thousand Cuban soldiers and fifty thousand civilians in supporting roles had participated in this war effort. Over two thousand young Cubans had died in Angola. Unlike the lonely and unheralded return of US soldiers from Vietnam, Cuba received her victorious heroes with parades and speeches. Raul Castro, Cuba's defense minister, spoke of the close friendship of the

Cuban and Angolan peoples as "ties of solidarity sealed in blood." Given that the likely point of origin of the AIDS epidemic in Cuba was Angola, those words seemed chillingly prophetic.

"I *was* proud of him, Elena," Cari told me. "But mostly I was just happy he was home. He came home on January twenty-first. He had to stay in the army hospital for a few days for some tests, and then he came home."

Cari paused and then reached out for the tape recorder and pressed the STOP button. Tears glistened in the corners of her eyes.

"Do you want to stop?" I asked softly.

"Just for a minute, maybe. This part is hard to talk about. I don't like to talk about it."

I waited quietly, uncomfortable and unsure what to do. I didn't want to push Cari beyond where she wanted to go just to get a "story." I wasn't a journalist, after all—I was a friend and a colleague. And I understood in a visceral way how hard this was to talk about. It had taken me years to tell my own story without fearing judgment from the listener—or that I would be overcome by my own emotions.

The rhythmic *thwak* of a worker's machete thinning weeds in the wooded area behind the house was the only sound.

Finally Cari began to speak again through silent tears. I pressed RECORD and listened.

"We were so happy to be together again," she said with a small smile. "We had been apart for two years. We had sexual relations as usual. It had been so long. A few weeks later, in February, the army contacted us and told us that Orlando might be carrying hepatitis B. They didn't say anything about AIDS at that time. No one said anything to us about AIDS."

Orlando was brought back to the army hospital for more tests. Caridad was again told that they were investigating him for hepatitis B, but she was already beginning to worry that something was being kept from her.

Caridad sat up straight in her chair and put her hands on the table, wringing them together as she continued.

"I was beginning to be suspicious, Elena, because I already knew a few things about AIDS, and I knew that it was an epidemic in that part of Africa. I started doing some checking about it on my own, with friends and colleagues, asking around. All that time, Orlando was hospitalized with the diagnosis of hepatitis B. Finally, in April, I went to see a doctor I knew at the Institute for Tropical Medicine. I explained that my husband was an Angola veteran who was hospitalized, and that I had also been sick with fever and diarrhea during the first week that he was at home. And that was when they finally did my test for HIV. I had to wait a couple of months for the news. The first two tests came back negative, but the third was positive."

Cari paused before her next words and then spoke in a strong, firm voice.

"I knew he must have had an affair in Africa and I wasn't happy about that, Elena, but he was my husband and I forgave him. One thing I am sure of—if Orlando had known that he had AIDS, I am sure that he would have done everything he could to not pass this infection on to me. We would have taken precautions. But as it happened, it was my turn, and I was the one to lose.

"On the thirtieth of April, 1986, they created this place, the sanatorium, and Orlando was the first to be admitted here. When my test came back positive in June of that year, I was also admitted. An epidemiologist and an army doctor came to my job, to my workplace, to give me my test results. They called ahead to let me know they were coming. At least they spoke with me privately there, not like has happened with some people at their workplace—and they told me that my test was positive and that I would have to enter the sanatorium."

Cari was given just a few days to put her life in order. Her family had to be told and arrangements made for her son. Cari's family helped right away without hesitation from the first moment that they learned of her diagnosis. Her parents cared for her son at first and then, in September of that year, José entered boarding school. "In more normal times," Cari said, "I don't think I would have sent him to boarding school."

The fact that Caridad had to send her son to boarding school was heartbreaking to me. It was hard enough for my kids and Clarence's daughter when he got sick, but at least we went through it together. This is what I had been trying to get across to Orlando in my first meeting with him. This policy that ended up separating families—it felt so unnecessary . . . and inhumane. On the other hand, so many of the kids I cared for in Newark were being raised by grandparents who had no support, financial or emotional, and were overwhelmed. In Cuba at least there was support for the family—a guaranteed income, free healthcare, housing, education. My mind was ping-ponging back and forth between these two opposing reactions. I wasn't sure how much more I could absorb.

"Puedo entrar?" A workman in overalls and hip boots stood at the door. It must have been his machete we had been hearing.

"Entra, Juancito. Entra!" Cari invited him in and gave him the customary Cuban greeting, a kiss on his dirty cheek. She got him a glass of water and asked if he wanted coffee. One thing I had always loved about Cuba is the way friendships and relationships transcended class and racial categories. Cari welcomed this workman into her home the same way she would have greeted a doctor who came to visit.

They talked in the kitchen for a few minutes, which gave me a chance to collect my thoughts. "Let's stop for a minute, Cari. I need to use the bathroom anyway."

I pressed the STOP button on the tape recorder and rose from the table slowly as Caridad went to ready the bathroom, stunned into silence by the weight of memories her story had stirred up. I too had waited to learn my fate after Clarence's diagnosis. I hadn't been tested myself until a couple of months after his initial life-threatening illness, unable to focus on anything but *his* struggle. When I finally went to Clarence's doctor to get tested, he told me I could expect results in about ten days. "Maybe longer if it's positive," he said. "That sometimes takes a little longer." I spent those ten days going back and forth to the hospital and went back to work part time. Clarence's mother and I fought gently over who would take care of him when he left the hospital. Clarence was slowly getting stronger—out of bed to the chair, a few steps down the hall with a walker. I woke up one morning and realized that two weeks had gone by and I hadn't heard from the doctor.

During that whole long wait, my thoughts see-sawed back and forth between hope and doom. One day I would wake up certain I was infected—why not? I thought this without worry, observing myself as if from a great distance. Then on another day, I would be convinced that I had been spared. Finally, I called the doctor. "Oh, Elena, I'm so sorry," he said casually. "Didn't I call you? Your results have been on my desk for a week. Your test is negative," he told me. I should have been angry after all that needless worry, but I wasn't sure how I felt—relieved, worried, guilty? Something in me wanted to share every part of this illness with Clarence. But for a couple of years, after several more negative test results, each time I had a scratchy throat or achy muscles, I felt just a little shiver of fear.

Cari's story had a different ending, and this was the crucial point at which our paths diverged in the road we had each traveled through this terrible epidemic. She herself was infected with the virus, while I was left to ponder, as I would many times, *Why her, why not me?*

When I came back from the bathroom, Juan was gone. We settled at the table again, and Caridad resumed her story as if there had been no interruption. She seemed eager then to share the whole of her experience with me, as if she would find new meaning in the telling. She seemed ready to go on, so I would too. Caridad began to describe what the sanatorium was like when she first arrived. She and Orlando were Patients Number One and Number Two.

"The conditions were very hard at the beginning. When you got here, they took your clothes and gave you a pair of pajamas and a towel. This was to keep you from escaping, from trying to go to the street in your own clothes. There is a video that was made about the sanatorium at that time and distributed in the US, and I was wearing the hospital pajamas in the video—and every time I see it, I think how ugly, how sad it was. I felt very closed in. We were living in a dormitory. I lived in a room with eight other women. There were several other rooms with four women in each. Altogether we were thirty-four women and we shared one bathroom—just a regular bathroom with one toilet and a sink and a shower for thirty-four women. On Sundays we took turns using the iron. We ironed pleats into our pajamas to look our best for our visitors."

I had only known Caridad a short time, but I could imagine how difficult the conditions she was describing must have been for her. I saw how much care she took with her appearance when we went out with the Prevention Group to do educational programs in the community. I could see how much pride she took in her home. The indignity of not being able to wear her own clothes, of having to share living space with so many others, must have caused her much suffering.

Visits were limited, she went on to tell me—only the immediate family, meaning mother, father, brother, son, only three visitors at a time. "I remember one Sunday I had a visit from my son, my mother, and one of my brothers. Another brother arrived at the gate and we both began to cry—he was not allowed to visit because I'd already had my three visitors."

"What about Orlando? Were you able to visit with him?" I asked quietly, family separation weighing on my mind again.

"I wasn't even allowed to stay in the same area as my husband. I had no contact with him at first except for very limited visits," Cari responded.

This pain, of being separated from Orlando, was the hardest to bear. They had been married for eleven years and had a stable and loving relationship. Though she was angry at first when she realized that the most likely explanation for his infection with HIV was infidelity during his time in Angola, Cari quickly forgave him and never thought about leaving him. At night, unable to sleep in her crowded dormitory room, she ached to be with him. Bed checks were carried out with flashlights to be sure that everyone was abiding by the rules. Even so, as Cari told it, some found a way to be together, stealing away to the hills to make love.

"But you know me, Elena," she said. "I was not going into the hills." We both laughed at the image of this intensely private woman sneaking away like a teenager, and the mood in the kitchen lightened for a moment.

"So how did things change, Cari? It seems so different now." I had visited openly-gay couples living together in the sanatorium. Transvestites wore what they liked and raucous drag shows were held on Saturday nights. It wasn't paradise—there were still lots of restrictions on patient activity and movement—but it was certainly very different from the locked-down hospital that Cari was describing.

"Do you know that we wrote a letter to Fidel?" Cari said with pride. "We were determined to make things better. We had a virus, but we were not criminals. We accept being here for the good of society, but we are not going to die in a few months. We have a right to live like human beings. That's what we told him."

Cari recalled meetings with the administration, letters and petitions to high government officials, and finally, the letter addressed to Fidel.

Changes occurred slowly. Dr. Jorge Perez, the director, was a staunch advocate for his patients, taking on the bureaucrats in the

Ministry of Health to fight for a more humane approach and one in keeping with what they had begun to understand about the virus. Private rooms were built for the married couples, then a theater and a video salon for entertainment. Caridad still found it hard to be forced to interact with so many different types of people at meals in the dining hall. Further petitions resulted in the creation of the neighborhood she now lives in, Marañon, with its private houses and kitchens where patients could prepare their own meals.

The rules governing visits outside the sanatorium also changed gradually in response to the persistent complaints of patients. Initially, patients were not allowed to leave under any circumstances. After several months, a policy was created that allowed visits with an *acompañante*, usually a doctor or medical student whose role it was to ensure that patients behaved in a way that did not threaten to spread infection when they were outside the walls of the sanatorium. Cari recalled visiting her son at boarding school with a doctor as her constant companion. "And if you went to the bathroom," she said with a laugh, "they stayed right outside waiting, in case you decided to escape through a window."

Finally, a system was created that allowed married couples to leave the sanatorium on visits without a companion. To take advantage of this privilege, some proof of the marriage had to be produced. Cari visited the hall of records to obtain her marriage certificate on one of her trips outside the institution. Only two couples living in the sanatorium were legally married at that time, but many wanted the privileges that came with marriage, so ceremonies were held where multiple couples exchanged wedding vows.

As Caridad finished her narrative of the early years of life in the sanatorium, she sat back in her chair and sighed. She seemed exhausted, as if she had relived every difficult moment. But it was with quiet conviction and in a strong, unwavering voice that she ended our discussion that day.

"I have always said that the worst thing that has happened to me in the last ten years was not being diagnosed HIV-positive, but rather it was being brought to the sanatorium in the way that I was," Cari related as she began to clear the table. "And if you asked me what is the best thing that has happened to me?" she went on, stopping at the sink and turning to face me. "It is knowing the people that I have come to know here, who have helped me to recapture my sense of humanity."

It was quiet when Caridad and I walked back so I could catch the workers' bus back to Havana. Norma was no longer in her rocker on the porch, and the domino players were gone from the front of their small apartment complex. We walked without speaking for a while, both lost in reflection as we stepped slowly along the path and under the tunnel. Finally, Cari broke the silence. "I have told you so much today, Elena," she said, stopping for a minute as we approached the long driveway out of the sanatorium where the bus was waiting, "because I feel close to you. It's like we are tied together by loss." We hugged, and I could feel her straight back relax just a bit through her thin cotton blouse.

"Gracias, compañera," I said as I boarded the bus, my Spanish not equal to the task of expressing the deep emotions I was experiencing in that moment. "I feel the same way. We'll talk again soon."

My long friendship with Caridad began in this house in the Marañon neighborhood of the sanatorium. She and her husband were among the first patients admitted in 1985.

CHAPTER SEVEN

LET THERE BE LIGHT BULBS

"*Me voy a las tiendas hoy.* I'm going shopping," I told Ruki after we'd finished cleaning the rice. It was Saturday—no work at the sanatorium that day. I would visit one of Havana's "dollar" stores to buy a few items for my room.

I'd purchased a bright red, Chinese-made "Flying Pigeon" bicycle from one of Miguel's friends. I retrieved it from the garage next to the house, where a trio of weathered amateur mechanics seemed to always be fixing the same 1956 Chevrolet, one of the many vintage cars that served as cabs and family transportation in Havana. "*Ciao, bonita. Buen viaje!*" They called out a friendly greeting as I wheeled my bike away from the curb, trying not to look as awkward as I felt.

What did the ordinary Cubans I passed on the street make of me, I wondered? What did they see? A middle-aged, determined-looking *gringa* with wavy auburn hair pulled back in a ponytail under a well-worn Brooklyn Dodgers cap. Certainly not a tourist? Not wanting to stand out, I wore the same pressed jeans and T-shirts that most Cuban women wore on the street, but my plump, well-fed frame and scuffed Reeboks gave me away.

My Chinese bicycle was heavy and had only one gear (definitely not *flying*), so I huffed and puffed as I headed up one of Havana's many hills. Bikes were everywhere in this city. In 1991, when fuel shortages made bus and car transportation costly and unreliable, Cuba had imported a million bicycles from China, and Fidel had exhorted the population to start pedaling. In 1996, bikes outnumbered cars and buses by twenty to one. It was not unusual to see a family of four teetering along on one bike—Papi pedaling, Mami on the front bar, and two kids bringing up the rear. I once saw a multi-tiered wedding cake being transported on a bike, balanced precariously in the hands of a woman sitting on the rear fender.

Potholes, diesel fuel, blistering heat, rambunctious Cuban cyclists, no helmets, no bells—my past biking experience had not prepared me for all of this. A Cuban doctor friend told me that when thousands of bikes appeared on the streets almost overnight, there was a dramatic increase in head-injury cases in hospital emergency rooms. Bike lanes were created, and the government started safety classes, but I still held on for dear life as young Cuban cyclists wove in and out of traffic, whistling or hissing a warning as they zipped past me. I arrived everywhere sweaty, red-faced, and breathless. But I did get a little extra credit for being *una norteamericana* brave enough to move around the city on a Flying Pigeon.

My destination that Saturday was a dollar store in Miramar where I hoped to buy a light bulb for my room. The single bulb, in the middle of my very high ceiling, didn't provide enough light for me to read or work at night. With U.S. dollars, I thought, it shouldn't be too hard to find a replacement. And I'd buy a few extra bulbs for Ruki. The house had only a few functioning light bulbs that were moved from room to room as needed.

I pedaled through residential neighborhoods that had very little visible commerce. The few billboards I passed proclaimed revolutionary slogans— *Hasta la Victoria Siempre* (Until the Final Victory) with an iconic portrait of Che Guevara, *Patria o Muerte, Venceremos* (Country or Death, We Will Win)—or encouraged Cubans to *Superar* or overcome one challenging situation or another. It was interesting to me that, contrary to what one might expect from the reverence with which Fidel was regarded, there were no posters or statues in his likeness. There was no cult of personality for Fidel or the living heroes of the revolution on display.

The only stores I saw as I pedaled the wide avenue were state-run *bodegas* or half-empty shops selling clothing, shoes, and a meager assortment of shampoos, cleaning fluids, and detergent. There were no street vendors—no young kids selling *chicle* or home-made sweets, no old men with colorful pillows of cotton candy on long poles as I saw everywhere in Mexico City or Managua. I was reminded, once again, that just about everything in this large, bustling city was run or carefully controlled by the state. There was a black market, which was growing during these hard economic times, but it seemed very random, not something you could count on to meet your needs. One night walking by the Malecón, I had been approached by a man dressed in a suit and carrying a briefcase. *Hamburguesa?* he asked, opening his case to reveal a dozen still warm hamburgers on buns that he was offering for sale. A few minutes later a man in paint-spattered overalls passed by. "*Cemento, cemento blanco,*" he muttered every few feet, drumming up customers for his product—white cement.

On the Puente de Hierro, an old iron bridge, my eyes wandered to the ramshackle wooden fishing boats that lined the piers below me as I struggled to keep my wheels straight on the hatched metal grid. The Rio Almendares wound through Havana, separating my neighborhood of Vedado from the more suburban one where the dollar store was located. It was a relief to come off the bridge onto the shady streets of Miramar, lined with the once-grand mansions of wealthy Cubans who had fled after the Revolution. They had been repurposed to house multiple families, cultural institutions, schools, and government offices.

The dollar store I was looking for was known as the *Diplotienda*, because it used to be open only to foreign diplomats and their families. Until 1994, it was illegal for Cubans to have dollars, and I used to see Cubans hanging around in front of this store, asking tourists to make purchases for them. By 1996, spending dollars was legal for Cubans. In fact, Cuban pesos were useful only to purchase those few staple food items that were available at the Cuban markets. For almost everything else, because of the dual currency setup, dollars were needed.

The Diplotienda had a special electronics and appliance section, and that is where I went in search of my light bulb. A young Cuban couple was wandering among the gleaming washing machines, refrigerators, and stoves. They must have relatives in Miami who send them money, I thought, if they are really planning on buying here. All of my Cuban friends were making do with antiquated Russian refrigerators and washers that were purchased in a different era, when the reward for being an outstanding worker or student was the chance to buy a cheap new appliance.

The word for light bulb was *bombilla*. I had looked it up before I left the house, not trusting my still awkward Spanish. I didn't want to repeat any of my widely celebrated language errors, like telling a roomful of people at a party that I was *jodia* instead of *Judia* in response to questions about my ethnic background. *Judia* means Jewish. *Jodia*, to put it in its most polite form, means all screwed up. To make matters worse, in apologizing profusely for my mistake, I had declared repeatedly that I was *muy, muy embarassada* (instead of *avergonzada*, a word I didn't know at the time). My Cuban friends got a kick out of repeating this story and teasing me about why I had never told them I was very, very pregnant.

When my turn came at the counter, I asked for my *bombilla,* but alas the store only had forty-watt light bulbs. I knew that this would not provide enough light for me to read and work, but the salesman was doubtful that I would find any more powerful in all of Havana. He insisted on proving to me that his light bulbs worked by plugging them into an electric socket set up behind the counter. It made perfect sense to test the light bulbs in a country in which so many things didn't work and couldn't be easily replaced. I decided to try another store.

At the third dollar store I visited, I finally located hundred-watt light bulbs and bought a good supply, pretested to be sure they were all working. I arrived home just in time to join the family for a dinner of rice, beans, and a small portion of meat that had been obtained with the weekly ration. After dinner, I unwrapped the light bulbs and was greeted like a soldier returning with the spoils of war. Ruki bounced on her heels with excitement, trying to decide where to place the bulbs in the apartment. She selected a lamp in her bedroom and one in the living room, and the rest were carefully wrapped and put away for future use.

Ruki's son Miguel was amused by my efforts to navigate the trials and tribulations of daily life in Havana. He spent his days tinkering with old radios and other small appliances in a room off the main foyer of the apartment. Miguel had graduated from a technical/vocational school with a certificate in radio repair and worked for a while in a state-owned repair shop. Several months before my arrival in the household, he had left this job. Like many young Cubans in the current economic crisis, he was finding it hard to see the benefit of working for the state. The salary offered him in Cuban pesos was not enough to offset the difficulties he encountered just getting to work each day and making sure he had something for lunch. In the past, the midday meal was provided at most workplaces, and public transportation functioned well. During the "special period" it was not uncommon for people to spend a couple of hours traveling to and from work and to have to make do with a meager lunch brought from home, or with nothing at all. Miguel, like many of his peers, was looking for another way to make a living. His small bedroom had been converted to a workshop from which he emerged at intervals each day spattered with oil and grease. Occasionally, someone from the neighborhood brought him a radio or toaster to fix. I never saw any money change hands, but a dozen eggs or a liter of milk occasionally appeared as payment.

Some of Miguel's young friends had already left Cuba on rafts. Despite his frequent complaints about the lack of opportunity to "get ahead" in Cuba, Miguel had no interest in joining them. Impressions of life in the US gleaned from Miami TV shows pirated in on satellite dish were enough to convince him that life on his peaceful island was preferable to the violent, crime-ridden streets of an American metropolis. He would stay put and continue to *inventar*, an all-purpose word for the creative adjustment that survival in Cuba demanded.

Miguel ambled into my room after dinner and balanced his tall lean frame on a chair to screw my hundred-watt bulb into the ceiling fixture. As we stood back to admire the way the beam of light illuminated my room, his gaze shifted to the large black duffel bag gathering dust in a corner. It held thousands of condoms I had collected from several different AIDS organizations in the US to be donated to the Prevention Group at the sanatorium. The special ceremony to acknowledge the donation had yet to be set up, though they were badly needed. Cuba was importing condoms from China and many Cuban men joked that they couldn't use the Chinese condoms because they were "too small." Condoms were probably more frequently blown up and used as birthday balloons than to prevent STDs.

When I had first arrived, Miguel and I had a laugh together as I shared my story of bringing them into the country. When I came through Cuban customs, a very solemn young official in military uniform had asked me the purpose of my trip. "Research," I answered. "I will be doing public health research."

"Please open the bag," he instructed, pointing to the overstuffed duffel on the counter. As I zipped it open, dozens of colorfully wrapped condoms began to spill onto the table. "Excuse me, miss, but exactly what type of research will you be doing?" he quizzed, his serious demeanor softened with a wink and a grin.

Now Miguel wanted to know if he could "borrow" a few of my condoms. "Do you need me to show you how to use them?" I asked.

"Oh, no!" he replied quickly, his olive complexion reddening with a nervous blush. And then a few moments later—"Well, if you want to, sure." Miguel watched intently as I expertly remove a condom from its packet and slowly and carefully unrolled it on my fingers. "Can you get AIDS from just one time?" he asked. Miguel, a good-looking young man with curly brown hair and a deep dimple in each cheek, had had a brief fling with an older, more experienced woman, and now he was worried. I give him the condoms and some literature in Spanish. Another prevention lesson in Cuba!

"Why did you want to come to Cuba to work with the *sidosas*?" Ruki asked that night, stopping in my doorway on her way to bed.

"You know how much I love Cuba," I said, "I'll take any chance to get back here. And I have a lot to learn." I knew that Ruki was both curious and frightened. The *sidosas*, as people with AIDS were often called in Cuba, had been living in isolated residential sanatoriums away from their communities for almost ten years, and the number of people with HIV/AIDS was still very small, so everyday Cubans didn't know a lot about the disease. Though it was not really a *secret* and people were aware if a family member or neighbor was living in the sanatorium, AIDS was not talked about much on the streets or in the homes of Havana.

"Aren't you afraid?" Ruki's question broke into my thoughts. I was afraid, yes, but not in the way she meant. I worried every day that I wouldn't be up to the challenge of teaching, that my Spanish wouldn't be good enough, that I wouldn't be able to bridge the cultural gaps that arose. What were people thinking of me? Would my contribution be enough?

I reminded Ruki of all the years I spent taking care of babies and children with this disease. "I've been doing it for so long I guess I don't think about it," I said, but she was already moving slowly away toward the bathroom, her arthritic limbs stiff at the end of a long day.

"*Bueno, Elenita,*" she yawned, tossing a goodnight over her shoulder. "*Mañana es otro día.*" Tomorrow is another day.

I cleared my bed of work papers, stretched out, and pulled the threadbare, much washed sheet over my tired body. The street was quiet now, but my swirling thoughts kept me awake. Why come to Cuba, Ruki had asked. Every Cuban I met asked me some variation of this question, trying to fathom why an American woman would volunteer to live and work in Cuba. I love Cuba, I told them, but this answer was starting to feel unsatisfying, incomplete. I had found adventure here, it's true, and even romance, though right now I was frustrated with that. I had been drawn to the spark of idealism that still felt alive on this island, despite all of the contradictions and problems. The *intention* to create a society that works for the common good, rather than the individual good, awakened my own sense of purpose and hope. I had been fascinated by all the paradoxes of Cuba, big and small—the sense of being frozen in time, yet full of life. When I was here, my "real" life melted away. I was out of touch and far away from all that was familiar and I became a different person—a leaner, sun-browned explorer in a new world, speaking a new language.

I had returned to this island over and over at times of transition in my life—following divorce, a career change, the death of my husband—and my visits had given me new energy to move forward. But how could I convey this to Ruki and Miguel and my other Cuban friends who lived every day with food rationing and blackouts? It seemed cavalier, even arrogant, to just keep repeating how much I loved Cuba.

Finally weariness overtook me. A soft breeze stirred the branches of the large tree outside my window, a bird whose name I had not yet learned called softly in the night, and I drifted off to sleep. Mañana es otro día.

CHAPTER EIGHT

A LONG JOURNEY HOME

I was glad when Alejandro, one of the leaders of the AIDS Prevention Group, accepted my invitation to lunch at Ruki's one Saturday when we both finally had an afternoon free. He couldn't participate in the peer-educator classes at the sanatorium every day because he had a full-time job, but it was obvious that his opinion counted. Often he breezed in at the end of a session, full of nervous energy, and everyone crowded around to talk to him. I wanted to get to know him better and to hear more about his story. How had this energetic, educated, opinionated young man come to be involved in this work?

After a lunch of stewed chicken, rice, and beans, we settled in to talk on the edge of my bed with the tape recorder perched between us. Alejandro had heard that I was interviewing some residents of the sanatorium for my fieldwork project and didn't want to be left out. "I will be open with you about everything, Elena," he told me with his customary enthusiasm. "I have nothing to hide." Ruki hovered in the doorway for a few minutes, perhaps uncomfortable with my entertaining a young handsome man in my bedroom, and then shuffled off to make us some café.

Alejandro was short, with a stocky build even in those days of food scarcity when many were trimming down. The Spanish roots of his surname, his pale coloring, and straight black hair reflected his ancestry—his maternal grandfather had come to Cuba from Galicia, Spain—but his manner of speaking was 100 percent Cuban, fast, loud, and full of gesticulations. He added emphasis to each declaration by slicing the air with his hands.

Alejandro was a whiz at computers and dedicated to his work in the Information Technology Department at the Institute for Tropical Medicine, a specialty hospital and research center that treated many of Cuba's AIDS patients. I knew he was one of the founding members of the Grupo de Prevención, but I didn't know much else about him. As Ruki appeared, rattling small cups of dark coffee on a tray, Alejandro signaled me to start recording and launched into his story.

"At the age of seventeen," Alejandro began, "I was chosen to study nuclear chemistry in the Soviet Union." It was quite an honor for him to have been chosen, and although it would be his first time so far away from his family, he was proud and excited by the opportunity. His family was proud of him too, though it was hard to think of him in another country, and for so long. Everyone came to the airport see him off on this exciting journey.

At that time, in the early 1980s, thousands of young people left Cuba every year to study math, chemistry, engineering, biochemistry, and other technical courses in Moscow. Cuba's relationship with the Soviet Union had been one of favored-nation trading status and economic dependence since the mid-sixties. It was a time of abundance in Cuba—pantries well-stocked with tinned meats, Russian-made TVs and refrigerators in every home, and Cuban highways filled with small LADA sedans. Alejandro's generation grew up studying Russian in school (emphasized over English, which was taught but not popular in those days) and the "Y" generation—the Yamilkas, Yamisleydis, Yuniors, and Yoannis, inspired by Russian names like Yevgeny, Yuri, and Yulia—played happily together in Cuban daycare centers, with a few Karls and Vladimirs thrown into the mix. The dissolution of the Soviet Union, which would have such a devastating impact on Cuba, was still several years away and did not affect Alejandro's daily life as a young student.

The time went by quickly. Though at first he was a little homesick for his family and his beloved island, Alejandro had adapted quickly to Moscow life and was thriving—making friends at the university and improving his Russian. He enjoyed being away from parental authority and, as a young gay man, he was taking full advantage of this freedom. Although homosexuality was stigmatized in the Soviet Union, as it was in Cuba at the time, Alejandro was able to socialize in a more anonymous environment where rumors and gossip could not hurt his family or his career. The risks were fewer, or so it seemed.

But suddenly his studies, his independence, and his carefree life came crashing to a halt when he found out he would be heading home six months ahead of time. He had been informed by a government representative that his father was gravely ill and handed a ticket for his return flight to Cuba that very same day. As he boarded the plane, he felt sad that this exciting experience was coming to an end, but most of all he was worried about his father and anxious to reach home and see his family.

The trip from Moscow to Havana was long but uneventful. He spent much of the time chatting with his seatmate—an older woman who was returning home to Cuba after several years of teaching medicine at Moscow University. They reminisced about all of the things they had missed about their homeland—the hot tropical sun and azure waters, the familiar plates of rice, beans, and fried plantains, the boisterous warmth of family and neighbors. For the last several hours of the flight, Alejandro dozed.

He awakened to the voice of the pilot announcing their descent and glimpsed his first view of Cuba through the tiny window—freshly ploughed fields, rows of royal palms, and then the airport—and on the upper balcony hundreds of Cubans waving their welcome and struggling for a better view of their family members as they disembarked. Grouped on the edge of the tarmac were several military jeeps and an ambulance.

"There must be somebody who is sick on this plane," he remembers remarking to his new friend. "And it must be someone important—there's an ambulance and some military vehicles down there waiting." With heightened concern about his father's condition, Alejandro gathered his things and prepared to leave the plane.

Halfway down the exit ramp he noticed them. Several men in military uniform had begun to make their way up the stairs. They reached him in minutes. One removed Alejandro's suitcase from his hand, the other began to guide him down the stairs and across the tarmac. "What's going on?" Alejandro asked, still thinking it had something to do with his father. "We'll explain when we get where we're going," one of the soldiers replied. No other information was offered and Alejandro did not ask any other questions. His uneasiness grew with each step. In a few short minutes, his life would be changed entirely by the dramatic news he was to receive.

"They didn't prepare me at all for the news," Alejandro recalled, his voice shaking as he reached this part of his narrative. Ruki moved into the room quietly to take away our coffee cups, but we paid her no mind. We were lost in the story.

"They took me to a little room at the airport that is used by the military, sat me down, and just told me like this: 'You have AIDS. It was discovered when you donated blood in the Soviet Union for the victims of Chernobyl. You will be taken to a hospital and you will be cared for. You probably don't have long to live. Don't worry about your things. We will have them sent from the Soviet Union.'" Alejandro paused for a moment, shaking his head at the memory. Through the open wooden shutters of my windows, we could hear the sounds of neighbors calling out to one another, a noisy car backfiring its way up the block.

"I didn't know what to think," he said. "I was in total shock. It was true I had donated blood in Moscow in a blood drive at the university, but no one had told me anything. I knew nothing about AIDS, just that it was a really bad disease that killed you. How could this be true, what would happen to me now? And how could they have been so cruel as to tell me my father was sick—to tell me that lie?"

The year was 1988, and Alejandro was eventually admitted to the sanatorium. In the length of an air flight from Moscow to Havana, his life had been transformed—he had gone from being an enthusiastic young student enjoying an international adventure to being one of Cuba's first AIDS patients, now relegated to life at Los Cocos.

Alejandro's story was not the first I had heard about the harsh methods that were sometimes employed in the early years of implementing Cuba's AIDS policy. Both public health officials and people living with HIV in Cuba acknowledged that fear and ignorance had created situations where privacy and basic dignity were violated. Military personnel or public health workers with little knowledge about the disease were dispatched to workplaces or schools to pick people up, informing them of their diagnosis and the need to enter the sanatorium in the same moment. Little effort was made to respect confidentiality, nor was there much understanding of the need for counseling and support. Almost everyone who received his or her diagnosis in those first couple of years had a painful story to tell. And almost everyone agreed that the errors of the past had been corrected. Many, like Alejandro, were now active participants in the fight against AIDS, choosing to contribute to the government's prevention efforts.

I also knew from my own experience that Cuba was not unique in stories that reflect overreaction, fear, and mistreatment of people with HIV/AIDS. The same year that Alejandro was given his diagnosis in that small room at the airport, my husband, Clarence, received the news in a Catholic hospital in Jersey City, New Jersey. As he battled a life-threatening infection, he was forced to lie on a hard stretcher in an emergency room cubicle for over forty-eight hours because there was no isolation room available for him. The hospital refused to admit him to a single room on the unit, insisting that he wait to be placed in a special double-isolation room reserved for TB patients. Food trays were routinely left outside his room and hospital personnel wore gowns, gloves, and masks to carry out even the simplest procedure like taking his temperature or blood pressure. It was a volunteer from the local gay men's HIV advocacy network—not the hospital social worker who never visited—who sat with me while I called the doctor to get the results of my own HIV test and then listened as I poured out my relief and fear. Two years later, when we found ourselves back in that same hospital, policy and attitudes had changed, but the change was hard-won and slow in coming.

"Ay, Elena!" Alejandro said, breaking into my thoughts and looking at his watch. "I didn't realize how late it is getting. I promised my mother I would stop at the 'Shopping' on the way home and see if they have any powdered milk."

"Go, of course, you should go," I said, turning off the tape recorder and sliding off the bed. I knew how important and endless the search for basic food staples was, more important certainly than reliving one of the most painful moments of his young life.

"Why don't you come for dinner next Saturday? You can meet my family and my boyfriend. And we can talk some more. Do you like pork? My boyfriend is a great cook." We agreed—next Saturday we would continue our conversation.

I didn't see Alejandro during the week, but he called Saturday morning to remind me that I had promised to come to dinner and to give me his address. I decided to take a Panataxi since his directions for bus travel sounded complicated. Traversing Santo Suarez, the hilly neighborhood that stretches to the north and west of the historic old city, in a cab made me very glad I had not tried to do this trip on my *Flying Pigeon*. The cab driver got lost, but after much stopping and asking, pointing and staring (at me in the back of the cab), we finally pulled up in front of the small, two-story house that Alejandro's family had called home for four generations.

Alejandro lived with his mother, two sisters, and assorted nieces and nephews in this house that his grandfather, the Spaniard, had built in first quarter of the century. Before the revolution in 1959, Santo Suarez had been home to middle-class homeowners, and his family had lived there since that time. Alejandro's mother had been a pharmacist who owned her own drugstore around the corner from their home. The revolution brought many changes, including the conversion of the drugstore to a state-run enterprise. The family home was also impacted by the revolutionary process. Prior to the revolution, Alejandro's family had owned the entire house and rented the first floor out to another family. After the revolution, the first floor became the property of the family that lived there. Alejandro's family continued to live on the top floor. Another family rented the floor below and yet another occupied a set of rooms tacked on at the back.

"Walk carefully," Alejandro warned. "Watch the cans." The house seemed to be in a state of frenzied repair—painting, plastering, rebuilding. Paint cans lined the stairs, the kitchen had been largely dismantled, and every wall bore traces of fresh paint and plaster. Painting and fixing up one's home was a luxury requiring access to US dollars in the Cuba of the 1990s. This project, whose frantic pace was dictated by the availability of materials, had been made possible by the generosity of an uncle living in Florida, Alejandro told me.

An enormous tropical fish tank, immaculately maintained, with coral and sea plants plucked from the Caribbean, dominated the living room. This was the first I had seen in a Cuban home; it was Alejandro's favorite hobby, which he had managed to sustain despite the difficulty of obtaining fish and supplies.

A pair of frantically barking dachshunds greeted my arrival at the top of the steps. Ochi and Cindy were the first well-fed, healthy-looking dogs I had seen in Cuba. There was no pet food available, and dogs were traditionally fed table scraps—but Cuban tables provided lean pickings. Those who did own pets had to employ creative strategies to keep them fed. At the sanatorium, after lunch in the dining hall, some staff members filled plastic bags with the remains of the meal to take home to their dogs. In my daily bicycle trips around the city, I had grown accustomed to being chased by the street dogs of Havana, which somehow managed to scavenge and survive. They looked like creatures assembled from a Dr. Seuss menagerie—scrawny and scruffy with strange topknots, fringes, and bald spots.

Alejandro's boyfriend, Javier, came to greet me with a warm smile and a hug. Shirtless and barefoot, he was younger than Alejandro and *muy guapo,* very handsome. I had heard the rumors around the sanatorium of Alejandro's reputation for playing the field, but this was a scene of cozy domesticity. I handed over a bag of the fragrant, dark espresso coffee that Alejandro had told me his mother loved—it was often unavailable in the Cuban markets—and Javier moved to the kitchen to prepare it for us.

While Javier made the coffee, Alejandro proudly showed me the master bedroom that they shared in his mother's house. The room, which opened onto the living room, was large and airy and lined with bookshelves. A queen-size bed took up most of the space, along with a desk that held a fairly recent model PC, fully equipped with modem and color printer—also a gift from the uncle in Florida. The only bathroom in the apartment was attached to and accessed through Alejandro and Javier's bedroom.

I was struck, as I so often was in Cuba, by the need to look beneath the surface to truly understand. Cuba was a country where words like *maricón,* which means "faggot," peppered regular conversation without raising eyebrows, where open homosexuals still could not join the Communist Party or work as teachers. And yet Alejandro and Javier shared the master bedroom in his home and seemed to be completely accepted as a couple by family and neighbors.

We gathered around a glass-topped table on the small terrace, pushing aside clothes drying on a line to set the table, and helped ourselves to heaping plates full of shiny black beans in rich sauce, garlicky pork roast falling off the bone, and the caramelized sweetness of ripe yellow plantains. The dogs sniffed around our feet hoping for an errant scrap, occasionally jumping up and then slinking away to a corner in response to Alejandro's stern, "No!"

Alejandro's mother, a thin, white-haired, nut-brown woman about a decade older than me, tall and straight in her flowered *bata de casa*, was interested in my work and my life at home. Unlike Ruki, she was still working, as a researcher in a biomedical lab, and took a great interest in Alejandro's work with the Prevention Group. Everyone called her "Mam*á*"—reminding me, with a pang of nostalgia, of Clarence's mom, who was "Mommie" to her whole neighborhood.

After dinner, Alejandro excused himself to work on something in the bedroom. Because he had a personal computer, a rare luxury in Cuba, Alejandro provided the group's email contact with other AIDS advocacy groups around the world, and produced much of the group's education and outreach materials from his home. The evening of my visit was no exception. His young nieces and nephews gathered round as he put the finishing touches on a flyer for the workshop we would conduct at a youth center the following week. Javier fussed at him about bringing his work home and not getting enough rest. Javier was also HIV-positive, but wasn't involved in any of the group's activities.

Javier and Mam*á* worked around the construction debris in the small kitchen to produce yet another *cafécito* and a beautiful flan custard bathing in delicious golden liquid caramel that Javier had cooked in a tin can submerged in a pressure cooker on the stove.

He had spent most of the evening in the kitchen—cooking, clearing, washing dishes, helping Alejandro's mother clean the rice and prepare food for the next day. Much later in our friendship, years later, after many such dinners and a few more boyfriends till Alejandro found his lifelong partner, I would joke about how he liked his boyfriends barefoot in the kitchen—the pregnant part not being an option.

Mamá took me to her room and we drank our coffee together, perched on the edge of her single bed. She held my hand in hers. "I want to tell you how it was for me," she said, "when they took Alejandro away." She recounted the events of that day in a soft voice, gazing into my eyes, never letting go of my hand, about how the government officials came to her workplace, the lab, to let her know that Alejandro was being taken to the sanatorium. "At least they took me into a private room to tell me," she said, "not like they did with some people—just telling them in front of their coworkers, neighbors, everyone." Mama knew something about this disease and so did her coworkers at the lab—they were in the medical field after all—and she did not panic. She just thought about her only son, her bright beautiful boy, and vowed to support him in any way she could.

Again, I thought of Mommie, sitting by Clarence's bed in the ICU during his first terrible illness and saying to him, "Get up, Clarence. You got to get up. Just get up. You can't leave now. Get up." Later she would tell everyone how she told him to get up and he did, her voice cracking with love. She had already buried two sons and a daughter from other illnesses, and she wasn't ready to let go of this one. "I don't care what it is he's got," she said. "I don't care if it's AIDS or whatever it is. Whatever he's got, I got it too." She, too, was a proud white-haired woman who was determined that her only son would live.

I never got to talk more with Alejandro that night about his time in the sanatorium. Seeing him at home, surrounded by his family, it was hard to imagine that young twenty-one-year-old wearing the pajamas of a hospital patient, stripped of his studies, living in a crowded dormitory. Did he sit in front of the dorm at night smoking and playing dominoes with the others? Who were his friends? Did he begin to organize to change things, as I saw him doing now? When did he decide to *live*?

Just before I left Cuba, I got some answers. "Let me tell you the story of the clock," Alejandro said one day when we were sitting around the office in the sanatorium. "Have I told you this story before, *Mamashka?*" Mamashka was Alejandro's affectionate nickname for me, based on his time in the Soviet Union and my Russian heritage.

"No, I don't think so."

"Come," he said, leading me by the hand through the door of the Casona, the large colonial mansion that served as the administration building of the sanatorium.

When we got outside and stepped back from the building, which was surrounded by stone colonnades and a stone patio, he pointed up at the large clock attached to the cupola at the top of the structure.

"When I first got here, that clock was not moving, stopped, frozen," Alejandro went on. "It really bothered me. It felt like everything in our lives had stopped when we entered these gates. I would look up at it all the time and try to force it to move with my mind." I looked up and saw that the hands had changed position. The clock was moving, almost imperceptibly across the stone surface, but moving.

"I started asking people, 'Why doesn't the clock work? Why doesn't anyone fix it?'

"They told me, 'Oh, that hasn't ever worked. The pieces to repair it with are scattered all over the sanatorium.'" That was easy to imagine, from what I had learned already about the challenges of fixing things in Cuba.

"What did you do?" I asked. "It seems to be working now."

"I just went and rounded up all the spare parts, and I figured out a way to put it back together. I kept working at it until I made the clock run."

"Wow, that's impressive," I said.

"But that's not the end of the story," Alejandro said, pulling me back into the air-conditioned office. "After some years had passed, I ran into a friend at an event, someone I had known at the sanatorium. Maybe you know him, I think. The big tall black guy who is a doctor, a friend of Caridad's."

"Oh yes, I've had dinner with him at her house."

"Well, I was talking to him at this event, and this big strong guy tells me, 'You changed our lives' and begins to cry.

"'Who, me?' I said. 'But how?' And then he told me like this." Alejandro said, pulling himself up tall as if to mimic the size and strength of his doctor friend.

"'We were all so depressed at that time, trapped in the sanatorium, all we thought about was that we were going to die. And then this little *amiguito,* this young guy came along and just fixed the clock that had always been broken. You have no idea what you did for us. You made us feel that life could continue.'

"I began to cry myself," Alejandro said. "I had no idea that he and so many other patients were trapped in the sanatorium, depressed, thinking they were going to die."

Alejandro left the sanatorium in 1994, eight years after he had first been brought there with a military escort—but not before he had made even more waves than he did by fixing the clock. When he first got to the sanatorium, all of the patients lived together, dormitory style, in the Casona. The facility was not really set up to be a long-term residential institution. As the population grew, new buildings went up and Alejandro went to live in *Los Edificios,* a complex of dorm-like buildings in another area of the sanatorium. When they started construction on Marañón, the community of small apartments and single-family homes where Caridad and her husband had lived, Alejandro went to the director to ask for an apartment there. The director was a military man and he had reserved Marañón for the soldiers returning from Angola and their families.

"He didn't want gays to live there," Alejandro shared when he told me the story.

"'Well,' I said, 'I am a disciplined person. I work hard. I think I deserve a house in Marañón.'

"'Oh, too bad. Everything is already spoken for,' the director said. Then he thought for a minute. 'Oh, maybe there is one you could have. It's still empty. It's right past the tunnel at the entrance. Go see it and see if you like it.'

"So I went with my roommate. The apartment didn't have windows, it didn't have a door, it didn't have a working bathroom. My roommate began to cry. 'We are not going to reject this apartment,' I said. 'We are going to live in this apartment.'"

They went back to meet with the director. "What did you think of the apartment?" he said. "Did you like it?"

"*Me encanta.* I love it," Alejandro said.

"B-but you went to see it?" asked the director.

"Oh yes, the one with no windows. I love it."

"Can you move in today?" the director said, sure he had won the battle.

"Oh sure, today, yes I can."

And he did, just like that. Alejandro's friends helped him look for doors and windows and a toilet, and in three months they had fixed up that apartment.

"After that," Alejandro went on, winding down the story, "things changed, things got better."

But not good enough to hold him there. Alejandro was one of the first patients to take advantage of a new ambulatory care policy that went into effect in 1994. The new policy, recognizing that HIV was a chronic, long-term condition and that many people lived for years without symptoms, allowed most people in the sanatorium to choose whether they wished to remain there or return to their communities. HIV-positive individuals who were newly diagnosed in Cuba were permitted to choose whether to enter the sanatorium or remain living at home. A three-month period of orientation and HIV education in the sanatorium was encouraged for everyone but not required. A small number of people were still admitted to the sanatorium or kept there regardless of their personal wishes—if their behavior prior to diagnosis was such that they might put others at risk of infection. Among this group were some members of Cuba's punk/hippie fringe, the *frikis*, as well as some *jineteras* or prostitutes. (The word literally means female jockeys and refers to an informal form of prostitution, young Cuban women trading sex and companionship for food and clothing for their families.)

By 1994, there were a total of thirteen sanatoria, one in each Cuban province, ranging in size from three inhabitants to over three hundred. Cuba's policy had always included the commitment to maintain whatever apartment or house people had lived in outside the sanatorium, and people were now faced with the choice of leaving their home in the sanatorium to return to the outside community or staying where they were. For many this was a difficult choice. Life in the sanatorium provided them a comfortable house or apartment with air conditioning, guaranteed easy access to good, nutritional foods, high-quality and specialized medical care, and the support and understanding of friends and health workers. In 1996, two years after the policy went into effect, Cuban public health officials estimated that 75 percent of those offered the option to stay in their home communities had chosen to do so, while 80 percent of those already living in the sanatorium had chosen to stay there.

For many the choice to leave was not so easy. But not for Alejandro. He had lost the carefree years of his youth to this disease, but he was still a young, healthy man. He was ready to live his life. And he was ready to do it outside the gated, leafy retreat that was Los Cocos.

Alejandro's mother is fiercely proud of him. She reminds me of Clarence's mom who cared for him with unconditional love.

Despite his youth, Alejandro was a strong and dynamic presence in our group.

CHAPTER NINE
CAMPING WITH THE ENEMY

I was badly in need of a break after a couple of months of working at the sanatorium and feeling lonely without Tony, who had left for Mexico, when Ruki's youngest son, Miguel, invited me to go with him and some other friends to a Cuban *campismo*, or campground. One of his friends had been offered tickets for a weekend away as a reward for having a good work record in her factory. Ruki was too disabled by arthritis to make the trip, but she encouraged me to go along—to get out of the city and see what a Cuban vacation spot was like.

We were to leave early Saturday morning, so we spent all of Friday getting ready. Sheets and towels were washed by hand and hung out to dry on the rooftop clothesline. Ruki made me promise to check the roof every hour to be sure that the clothes would not be stolen. This kind of theft, once unheard of in Cuba, had been increasing as the economic crisis worsened. We prepared packages of all the food we would need for the weekend, as there would be nowhere to purchase anything along the way. Ruki packed some rice, tinned meat, eggs, and a few precious oranges in a duffel bag, along with a couple of pots to cook in. We woke at five o'clock and set out with our bundles to catch the bus.

By the time we arrived, a line had already formed at the corner where the buses were to pick us up. Miguel's friends greeted him warmly and gazed curiously at the *gringa* who accompanied him. When they realized I spoke Spanish, they immediately began to ply me with questions. *What did I think of Cuba? What was I doing here? Where did I live in the US? Did I know any Cubans in New Jersey? Was I married? Did I have children?*

Only one bus showed, instead of the two that were expected, but there was no way we were leaving anyone behind, so we all crammed aboard. The smallest and lightest sat on laps, while others took turns standing in the aisles for the entire two-hour trip to the coast. It was hot, even with the bus windows open, and the smells of sweat, cigarette smoke, and the food we were all carrying mingled in the stifling air. Finally, as the bus rounded a curve in the hilly road, we caught our first glimpse of the brilliant aquamarine Caribbean, and everyone cheered.

The campground was perched high on a rocky hill overlooking a small horseshoe-shaped cove. A sandy path wove between simple stone cabins and then down to the beach. Each cabin had bunk space for six, a small area for cooking, and a latrine. While Miguel and his friends busied themselves checking under the mattresses for hidden tarantulas, I wandered down to the beach. Later we prepared a lunch of rice and Spam, and then it was siesta time.

That night, after finishing off the leftover rice, we made our way over to the *discoteca*—a large wooden platform high on a hill overlooking the ocean. The night air was balmy, and the mosquitoes were not yet biting. Colored lights were strung on poles around the dance floor, and a local salsa band was shifting into high gear when we arrived. Miguel was shy and not a dancer, but one of his friends took me out on the floor for a merengue, much to the amusement and delight of the rest. Below us, the ocean was invisible in the darkness, except for an occasional white-capped wave and the sound of the surf crashing onto the beach. Far off in the distance, we could see a dotted line of lights bobbing in the water.

The band was at full throttle and the *baile* in full swing when the music suddenly stopped, and a man stepped to the microphone to make an announcement. "I am sorry to inform you," he began in a serious voice, "that we must stop the discoteca for the evening, and I must ask you to return to your cabins. There is a report of a security situation off shore, and we have been asked to observe a blackout here at the campgrounds."

Rumors flew through the crowd as we hurried back to our cabins, but no one had any real information. We spent the rest of the evening swatting mosquitoes on the front porch of our cabin and gazing out at the lights slowly moving up and down the coast.

In the morning, there was no newspaper to enlighten us about the events of the night before, and no further announcements were made as we headed home. When we arrived in the early afternoon, sandy, sweaty, and tired from our journey, Ruki met us at the door. "Elena, your family, your friends, they've been calling you." Ruki, who spoke little English, had managed to figure out that they were worried about me and were calling to make sure I was all right. We told her about the incident at the discoteca, but none of us had any idea what had really happened. There was no CNN to bring us instant reports. The newspaper *Granma* disappeared quickly from the newsstands and was mostly used as toilet paper. We would have to wait for the seven o'clock news.

The whole family gathered around the TV as the somber-faced Cuban news anchor brought us the first story of exactly what had occurred during the night we had spent at the campground. Three small planes from Florida had encroached on Cuban air space and ignored repeated warnings to turn around. This was not unusual. Brothers to the Rescue, a right-wing Cuban exile group in Florida, frequently sent planes in to pick up groups seeking to cross the Florida Straits on makeshift rafts. Other similar groups sometimes dropped leaflets over the island, urging Cuban citizens to rise up and overthrow the "Castro dictatorship." They never filed flight plans, and US authorities looked the other way. Cuba had endured years of espionage and attacks, ranging from mild provocations to full-scale invasions.

But the Cuban government had issued a strong warning several months earlier. A terror campaign was escalating, carried out by exile groups against Cuba's resort hotels with the objective of destroying the tourist industry by scaring the travelers away. One Italian tourist had recently been killed by a bomb in the lobby of his hotel. These incursions would no longer be tolerated. Planes that flew over the island in violation of international law would be shot down.

As the first test of this new edict, Cuban MIG fighter jets had pursued three small Cessna planes, warning them to turn around. Failing to heed the warning, two of the planes had been shot out of the air. The third had turned around. The lights we had seen moving up and down the coast were those of Cuban Coast Guard cutters searching for survivors. The four Cuban-Americans on board the planes were presumed dead. A full-scale international incident was unfolding, with dramatic rhetoric on both sides of the Florida Straits.

My mother had called three times. Other friends who spoke some Spanish called and were able to convey to Ruki their urgent need to speak with me. There was no way for me to return their calls from Ruki's phone, so I would just have to wait for them to call back.

I could only imagine how this was playing in the US—the constant barrage of breaking news, special reports, news analysis, and reactions from the Cuban exile groups in Miami, responses from President Clinton and from Congress. Cuba defended its action to the world by placing this incident in the context of the long history of attacks by exile groups, starting with the ill-fated Bay of Pigs invasion. Soon we learned that the president had announced an immediate tightening of the US economic embargo to punish Cuba for this "act of war." For those of us in the US who had been working for normal relations between our country and Cuba, this was a major setback. For Cuba it was just one more challenge to be overcome.

The following morning, my mother managed to get through. "I'm fine, Ma," I said, my voice echoing back in my ears. "Everything here is fine."

As I boarded the bus for work at the sanatorium, I was greeted by a flurry of questions and comments.

"Are you going to have to leave Cuba?" asked Alex, whose sister in Miami had called and raised his anxiety about the incident.

"Why does your government want to punish us? What have we ever done to them?" queried Adela, one of the kitchen workers.

Manolo, the maintenance worker who had warmed to me after he learned I had come to Cuba with the Venceremos Brigade, surprised me by his response. "You can't blame her for what her government does, Adelita. We don't hate the North American people. They are just ignorant."

I took a seat next to Andrea, a psychologist at the sanatorium, who shrugged philosophically. "Life goes on, Elena." she sighed. "We're used to this. We'll survive this, you'll see. We've survived worse than this."

And she was right. Life did go on. Cubans continued to walk out in the humid air of the early morning to buy their daily ration of bread, to queue up for the bus, to stroll along the Havana seawall in the moonlight, to take their kids to school. Life—busy, complicated, vibrant, noisy life—went on.

Hermes serious demeanor hid a tender and compassionate heart.

CHAPTER TEN

NINETY MILES OF SEPARATION

From the first time I had met Hermes several years earlier, I had been drawn to his air of sadness. He seemed like a quiet, calm island in the midst of the loud clamor of a typical Cuban gathering, and when he did speak he often hesitated, as if lost in thought. I was intrigued by what stories might lie beneath his reserve, so when he invited me to have lunch with him at his home in Havana, I eagerly accepted. He was the only member of the Prevention Group who had never lived in the sanatorium. What was his story? We had agreed on a Saturday when no other activities were planned.

I rode my bike, not wanting to wait on long lines or shoehorn myself into one of the few overcrowded buses on Havana's streets on the weekends, and parked it in front of the address Hermes had provided, locking it to a small tree. Hermes had explained that he lived on the roof of his building. I was looking up and wondering how I would get up there when he arrived to show me the way. We walked together up a poorly lit stairway to a worn and rusted ladder that led to the roof. To avoid an attack of dizziness I kept my eyes fixed on the cloudless sky above as I climbed.

The ladder took us to the tar roof of a four-story building with views of the hilly neighborhood stretching out around us. Hermes lived in a one-room, windowless cement-block dwelling. Crisscrossing wires brought electricity from the building below, and a propane tank fueled the small cookstove on which he busied himself preparing coffee. A small wooden table was neatly set with a colorful cloth, plates, and glasses for our lunch—a tuna and macaroni salad, white rice, and black beans. An occasional breeze through the open door provided the only ventilation as we sat around the table to eat and talk.

"Let me show you what Mami sent," Hermes said after we had finished our meal and he had stacked the dishes in his makeshift sink. A year earlier, when I was first introduced to Hermes, he had asked if he could put me in touch with his mother in Miami so she could send down a package for him the next time I came. I could hear the longing for her son in her voice when I called to give her my address, and her love for him was reflected in every item in her care package.

Hermes brought out the blue nylon duffel bag I had carried down for him to show me the treasures his mother had sent. A neat stack of striped polo shirts, a couple of pairs of ironed jeans, a pair of very white, brand-new tennis shoes, shaving cream, deodorant, men's cologne—all things that were so hard to find in Cuba. But the most important gift—a bag of AIDS medications she had collected from organizations in Miami. Most newer AIDS medications, kept out of Cuba by the U.S. embargo, were only available through these kinds of donations, though the Cuban government was working hard to develop their own medications and diagnostic tests. "These will save my life, Elena. Without these I cannot survive." Hermes held up a plastic Ziploc bag crammed with prescription bottles of antivirals and antibiotics, tubes of antifungal creams and lotions. American AIDS organizations were getting donations of medications when patients died and making them available for Cubans who had no other way to obtain them. Hermes's illness had progressed to the point that only the newest generation of AIDS meds, unavailable in Cuba, could help him. "The gift of life," he called it as he put the bag away. He brought out bowls of rich, sweet flan and small cups of dark espresso coffee for dessert.

When I had said good-bye to Hermes after the first time we met, I remembered thinking I might never see him again. He had been very ill off and on for a couple of years and hospitalized several times with serious infections. A year had passed, and he was painfully thin and fragile looking, his skin pale beneath its burnished copper color. But he was still here, thanks to his mother's love and his own strong will.

Hermes spoke in an even, almost melancholy tone, no matter what he was talking about. His rich, baritone voice seemed too big for his slight frame, but made it easy to imagine him as a radio announcer, which had been his profession before he was diagnosed with HIV in 1991. I found myself getting lost in the slow, deep rhythms of his speech as I turned on the tape recorder and he began to tell me his story.

Hermes's mother and younger brother had left Cuba for Miami when he was only eighteen, and his separation from them was still a painful undercurrent in his life. Originally he had hoped to join them in exile, but his father, a well-known hero of the revolution who had fought with Fidel and Che in the mountains, had refused to give his consent and Cuban law at that time required the consent of both parents up to the age of twenty-one, so Hermes had been left behind. He did not see his mother again for almost twelve years, and by that time he had been diagnosed with AIDS.

Family separation was a constant theme in the lives of Cubans, both on the island and in the US. In the early years after the revolution, hundreds of thousands of Cubans left the island—mainly the country's rich and middle classes who had the most to lose from the shift toward socialism. This community of exiles was welcomed with open arms and provided with a level of government assistance and

opportunities not afforded any other immigrant group. Most Cuban
emigrants settled in Miami, close enough to Cuba to keep alive their
dreams of a triumphant return.

Hermes's mother and brother were part of the second big wave
of Cuban emigration. In 1980, after a weeklong crisis during which
over ten thousand Cubans sought refuge in Havana's foreign embas-
sies, Fidel Castro announced that any Cuban who wanted to leave
the island could do so. About 125,000 Cubans took advantage of this
offer, assisted by a fleet of small boats from Miami, in what became
known as the "Mariel Boatlift." Among them were many less-than
voluntary-departures—homosexuals who felt pressured to leave,
mental patients, and prisoners released for the exodus. One Cuban
friend remembers being brought to the port of Mariel as a schoolgirl
and encouraged to hurl eggs and verbal insults at those who were
leaving. The joke on the island now is that the *Marielitos,* as they are
called, often return to visit their struggling families, bringing the gift
of a dozen eggs.

I had seen how this difficult history had driven a wedge into traditionally close Cuban families. In the US, the most intransigent of the
Cuban exiles have formed paramilitary groups and carried out espionage and attacks against Cuba in the hopes of fomenting a coun-
terrevolution. Other right-wing exile groups oppose providing any
type of aid to Cuba, even personal assistance to their own families.
And in Cuba, for many years, it was considered a liability to maintain
contact with family in Miami—a fact that, if discovered, could close
off certain opportunities for career advancement. This was definitely
the case for Hermes.

"At first, I only got letters," Hermes said of those first difficult years
after his mother's departure. "In those days it was frowned upon to
maintain any kind of communication with family members who had
left Cuba. Even though it was my mother, it was very complicated."
Phone calls were almost impossible, but Hermes made arrangements

with the grandmother of a childhood friend who allowed him to receive calls from his mother at her house. "But then it was like this," he went on. "The operator would call my friend's house to let them know a call would be placed. Then I would have to wait there, sometimes one or two days, waiting and waiting for her call—only to find out that my mother had been unable to place the call. If finally she was able to call, then it would be another twenty-four hours of waiting for the call to get through—so I would wait and wait again—and maybe the call would finally get through at two in the morning—and we would only be allowed to speak for three minutes!"

Hermes's diagnosis with HIV and his serious illness had given the relationship with his family in Miami a sense of life-and-death urgency. Hermes did not tell his mother about his diagnosis until almost a year after he received the news. "I didn't want to tell her at first," he said. "I thought she would feel so desperate, unable to help me, so far away. What could she do to help me from there? I felt so depressed, almost suicidal really. I thought to myself—am I going to die without ever seeing my mother again, or my little brother who I have never met?"

Once Hermes's mother was finally able to visit, she had managed to see him once a year, all that was allowed for Cuban-Americans under the US travel restrictions, but he had so far been unable to obtain a visa to visit her in Florida. In between visits, they maintained phone contact, and she used every available opportunity to send him medications and money with which he could supplement his diet and purchase necessities only available to those with dollars. The same US laws that restricted his mother's visits to the island also restricted the amount of money she was allowed to send him.

Hermes's mother worked in a beauty parlor in Hialeah, the center of the southern Florida exile community. She accepted all the overtime hours she could get and saved her money to buy AIDS medications for Hermes. From time to time she called me with a list of the medications Hermes needed—Bactrim to prevent PCP pneumonia which had hospitalized him more than once, Diflucan to fight the yeast infections that made it hard for him to eat, and protease inhibitors, the new miraculous antiviral drugs that were revolutionizing AIDS treatment. The US embargo created challenges for the Cuban Ministry of Health, which was committed to providing these life-saving medications to Cubans living with HIV/AIDS, and donations from family members and organizations outside of Cuba were often the only way these medications could be provided. Hermes's mother had managed to purchase a three-month supply of medication—could I help out by getting donations? Between us, we were able to guarantee that Hermes would have enough medication for six months. What would happen after that?

After our lunch that afternoon, Hermes and I stepped outside his room to stretch and get some air. Makeshift homes like Hermes's rooftop room were becoming increasingly common in Havana. Housing laws kept rent at no more than 10 percent of a person's annual income, and 80 percent of Cubans owned their own homes or apartments. But shortages of materials had brought new building and repairs to a grinding halt, and Havana was dotted with crumbling edifices and half-finished construction projects. High-ceilinged homes were transformed by the addition of sleeping lofts or *barbacoas* to accommodate family members who lived doubled- and tripled-up in small quarters. Signs offering *permutas,* or trades, of one large apartment for two smaller ones cropped up in windows throughout the city.

The housing shortage was one of the main reasons that many Cubans with HIV/AIDS had chosen to live in the AIDS sanatorium. But not Hermes. We returned to the table and settled in with another cup of coffee. Hermes circled back to the beginning of his story.

He was born, he told me as I inserted another tape cassette in my recorder, in 1961 in the province of Las Tunas in the central part of the island. Hermes's mother had been nineteen years old and unmarried, which at that time was scandalous. "Not like now," he added, with a knowing wink. Despite the scandal, she returned from Havana to her native province to give birth, assisted by the same midwife who had delivered her. Her family of rural peasants accepted her back into their lives and raised Hermes as if he were their own son.

Hermes Sr., Hermes's father, was a *comandante,* or commander, of the revolution who began his service with Fidel Castro in the Sierra Mountains at a very young age. Hermes related what I imagined was an often-told family tale of how his scrawny, thirteen-year-old father had to prove his strength by hoisting a huge bag of ammunition over his shoulder. Che Guevara, a revered hero of the Cuban revolution, was assigned to serve as a mentor to the young boy, and Hermes's mother first met his father through her connection to Che. She came from a family whose history of involvement in the revolutionary cause went back to the 1930s. They were members of the Cuban Communist Party when, as Hermes states, there were *"comunistas de verdad*—real communists, not like today when anybody can join the party."

Hermes's father did not acknowledge his paternity at first, but when he returned from a trip to the Soviet Union and saw his nine-month-old son for the first time, he could no longer deny being his father—they looked exactly alike. From that day on, Hermes's difficult and conflicted relationship with his famous father marked his life.

Hermes's voice softened with nostalgia as he told me about his happy childhood in the home of his grandparents in Las Tunas. He learned to read and write before he went to school, and his mother's family exposed him to a world of culture, books, and ideas. Hermes lived with them until he was seven years old, at which point his mother married another man, and he returned to live with them in Havana.

As a young teenager in Havana, Hermes chafed at being overprotected and sheltered—not allowed to do the things that other kids

did, like go to the beach or hang out at Havana's Malecón. He managed to slip away for some mischief-making from time to time. His
first sexual experience occurred during this period of his life, when
a girlfriend "seduced" him on the living room couch. As a prank, he
remembered once filling condoms with condensed milk and throwing them into parked cars. Now he couldn't imagine throwing away
milk that costs $1.40 a can, or condoms that were so hard to come by.

After his mother left Cuba looking for economic opportunities,
Hermes stayed in Havana and studied journalism but chose not to
complete a university degree because of his desire to emigrate. In
Cuba, a university education is free, but those who choose to leave
the country are required to pay an exit fee for the education they have
received.

Hermes entered the world of radio by chance. In the 1980s, he told
me, it was still possible to be evaluated based on one's skills, and to
get a position and start a career even without a degree. One night he
went to a party of intellectuals who worked in radio and was introduced to someone who gave him his start as an announcer.

Hermes began his career by working in a variety of radio stations,
some in Havana and some outside the city. By 1991 he had achieved a
good position at one of the capital's most important stations, and one
I was very familiar with as the background to my morning chores
with my landlady, Ruki. I could easily imagine Hermes's resonant
bass tones coming over the radio with great confidence and properly
rolled R's.

"I knew about AIDS then," Hermes said, "but I didn't think it
would touch me. I had a very apocalyptic idea about the disease. You
were infected—you died. That's how I thought about it." Like many
Cubans during that time period, Hermes believed that all who were
infected with HIV were sequestered in the sanatorium. "We didn't
talk about it at all," he explained. "People were afraid to even mention
the word."

Hermes had a blood problem, a genetic platelet disorder, and needed to have frequent blood-work to monitor it. An aunt who worked in a lab in the large maternity hospital in Havana regularly checked his blood for him. In November of 1990, when he went in for his routine blood-work, he asked to have an HIV test done—not for any particular reason, he said, just to do it. Hermes's HIV test was positive. He was informed of the results of that test in January of 1991, but was told that the test had been contaminated and had to be repeated. In reality, Hermes believes, that was just a way to soften the blow while the confirmatory Western blot test was performed. On February 5, 1991, authorities from the Ministry of Health informed him that his HIV test was positive. It was, he said ironically, "like a new birthday"—but one that he feared marked not life but the beginning of his death.

Hermes struggled with depression and despair during the months following his diagnosis. He stopped working, not because he had to, but because he had lost hope. "I had a feeling that I had no future," he explained. "I lived that way for a year. It was very, very difficult, but the hardest thing I could think of was to have to go to live in the sanatorium."

Hermes had never visited the sanatorium, nor did he know anyone who was living there, but the thought of being compelled to enter this institution was repugnant to him. At that time the program was mandatory, but the sanatorium in Havana was very full. Smaller residences were being constructed in each province so that patients could live close to their home communities. In six months, Hermes was told, there would be room for him in Havana and he would have to enter. "My idea of the sanatorium was that you went there until you died. I said to them, 'I'm sick. I haven't committed any crime. Why do I have to go to a prison?'"

For almost a year Hermes tried to come to terms with his diagnosis, but he couldn't shake the feeling that his life was over. At the end of that year, the health authorities approached him again about entering the sanatorium, but again he rejected this idea. "They came to my house and tried to convince me," Hermes said, "but I said I would not go on my own feet. They threatened to call the special police that enforce health policies. I very calmly got to my feet, opened the door, and said 'Go ahead and call them, because on my own feet I am not going.'" Hermes actually rose to his feet and strode to the door of the small room where we sat as he described this confrontation in a firm, deep voice, as if to convey the depth of his conviction. Because the policy of mandatory quarantine in the sanatorium was already beginning to change, and because of Hermes's insistence, the authorities left him alone.

Hermes's family was very helpful to him during this crisis. His mother stepped up her efforts to send him money during this time, cushioning Hermes's life in Cuba. Hermes acknowledged that this assistance had diminished his suffering during Cuba's economic crisis and made it possible for him to live with HIV outside the sanatorium. For many others, the sanatorium offered both emotional and material support that was otherwise difficult to access, and they had come to see it as a community and a home.

"I never saw it as a home," Hermes stated. "For me the most terrible thing was to have to go and live in that place—to leave my house, my friends. To live with people who didn't have anything to do with me, who I might not like or get along with."

Hermes's firm decision not to enter the sanatorium coincided with the policy change that made living in the sanatorium voluntary, and he was eventually allowed to remain permanently in his home community. Once the threat of being forced to live in the sanatorium was removed, Hermes began to spend time there of his own accord—to participate in support and education activities and to begin to reconstruct his life. When I first met him in 1996, he was traveling to the sanatorium every day to work in the

Psychology Department and had become an active member of the AIDS Prevention Group.

One day, several weeks after our discussion in his rooftop room, Hermes invited me to observe a prevention education session in Maríanao, a neighborhood on the outskirts of Havana. The event was being held at a community youth recreation center tucked into a residential block of square cement apartment buildings. The outdoor patio of the center was set up with folding chairs, and a loudspeaker on the corner broadcast a static-filled and almost incomprehensible invitation to the neighborhood. Hermes and a couple of other group members were setting up a long table in the front for the speakers. Today was to be the unveiling of what we had come to call the *pene de goma*—a larger-than-life rubber penis I had prevailed upon my daughter to purchase for us in a sex shop. "Ma, this is Cincinnati, not Greenwich Village," she had reminded me when I phoned to make my request. With great embarrassment she had bought not one, but two (one chocolate and one vanilla) erect rubber penises that would be used to demonstrate proper technique with a condom.

The event got off to a slow start, but finally about fifteen of the chairs were filled with young people from the neighborhood, and Hermes began a factual presentation in his deep announcer's voice. Caridad came from her apartment in Central Havana, and several other HIV-positive members of the Prevention Group sat behind the table with her. No personal stories were shared, just information about the virus and how to prevent transmission. One young woman who had spent most of the session laughing and talking with her boy-friend started the question period with a bang. "I thought everyone with this disease was living in Los Cocos," she began. "Now you're telling me anyone can have it and I have to be careful. I think if they are going to let people live out here, they should make them wear a mark or something so we will know who they are. I don't want to have to change my life just to keep from getting their sickness."

The group at the front table shifted in their seats. Hermes cleared his throat nervously and moved the microphone closer, but before he could begin to answer, an older woman in the audience stepped forward and grabbed the mike. "I cannot believe what I am hearing," she said, looking down the row at the young girl. "People with AIDS are sick; they need our sympathy, not our rejection. You cannot make someone else responsible for your health—you have to take the responsibility yourself. We all have to learn about this disease. That's what we are doing here today." She sat down. The young girl giggled nervously and resumed whispering to her boyfriend.

A lively condom relay race was held with the pene de goma, the rubber penises passing from hand to hand as the two teams struggled to follow each step in applying a condom and do it as fast as possible. By the end we had collapsed in laughter, and condoms were distributed as prizes for both the winning and the losing team. As dusk fell and the mosquitoes chased us inside, the afternoon ended with a showing of a bootleg copy of *Philadelphia*. About a dozen young people gathered around a small TV set in the center to watch the two-hour movie. At the end, when the character played by Tom Hanks lies dying surrounded by loving family and friends, everyone in this Cuban audience was crying openly, including the girl who suggested that people with HIV should wear marks of identification.

A week later, Hermes issued another invitation for me to observe his work at a public health center in the building that housed the Center for Epidemiology and Hygiene for Havana Province. Members of the AIDS Prevention Group ran peer-counseling sessions there twice a week for newly diagnosed HIV-positives. Hermes had learned from his own experience how important it was to get that kind of support, and he was an enthusiastic participant in the program.

The building was old, with tile-lined walls and floors and flickering fluorescent lighting. An antiseptic odor, reinforced by constant mopping, permeated the hallways. It was lunchtime when I arrived, and Hermes took advantage of the break to fill me in on the work of the peer counselors.

"It's so different from what happened when I received my diagnosis," he said. "I felt so alone. There was no one I could share my fears with." The peer-counseling program had been started a year earlier by the Prevention Group, and sessions were held on different days at a variety of sites around the city. I remembered the stories told to me by those who had been given their diagnosis by military personnel and then transported directly to the sanatorium. What a huge change these simple counseling sessions represented!

Though by 1996 this type of support was taken for granted in the US and was built into most HIV/AIDS programs, the early years of our own struggle with this disease were not so different. I remembered again my own experience in 1988, when a technician drew my blood with no counseling at all, and Clarence's doctor "forgot" to call me for two weeks to give me my results.

Lunch break was over, and Hermes and I returned to the small room where the next counseling session would take place. Several plastic chairs were placed around a wooden table. A couple of posters from the last international AIDS conference were taped to the otherwise bare and dingy walls. A young man walked hesitantly into the room and asked for Hermes. "My name is Diego," he said, "and I need to talk to someone." Hermes rose from his chair, shook Diego's hand, and put his arm over his shoulder.

I said my good-byes, happy that my friend had found the strength to use his misfortune to help others. Hermes's voice carried down the corridor after me. "*Bienvenido, hermano*," I heard him say. "You've come to the right place."

*Hermes and Caridad conduct a workshop with the
"Pene de Goma" at a neighborhood park.*

CHAPTER ELEVEN

SEARCHING FOR PIÑA IN HAVANA

Whenever I needed to decompress and escape for a while from the intensity of my work in the sanatorium, I visited my friend María Luisa, the actress whom I had met in 1991 during my Reality Tour trip to Cuba. We had remained good friends. In fact, she was the one who had introduced me to my boyfriend Tony, her cousin, which I tried not to hold against her as I waited in vain for a letter from him from Mexico!

I had been invited for a special occasion—the celebration of María Luisa's daughter (and my honorary niece) Lucía's fifth birthday—and had spent the morning scouring the neighborhood for ingredients needed to make an *ensalada fria*, a cold macaroni salad that María Luisa could offer to the aunts and cousins who would come to the small party.

In María Luisa's family, she had told me once, in a story that sounded like it could have been written by Gabriel García Márquez, there were fourteen women named María—a chain of Marías, beginning with her grandmother and descending down through her mother, her *tias* María Elena, María Juana, María del Carmen, María Ana, and María Julia, and finally to her, María Luisa, the littlest

María, now a mother herself. She had broken the chain when she named her baby daughter *Lucía*—a poetic name that she had always loved. I wondered how many of the Marías would make it to the birthday party as I trudged up the stairs to her apartment through the sticky air of a hot August day in Havana.

Lucía was playing with her friend Diana in the exterior hallway of the building. "Tía Elena," she called out to me as I passed. "*Encontraste el jamón?*" Did you find the ham? Even young Lucía understood how hard it was to find a piece of ham in Havana. Her father, Omar, had gone out on his bicycle to pick up a few things for the party, candy and cake that the family was entitled to purchase with their ration card. María Luisa's mother, María del Carmen—the second of the Marías—had stayed behind to clean the apartment and begin the preparations.

"Hola, Marí, I'm back." I was determinedly cheerful as I put down my bags on the counter of her small kitchen. I didn't want María Luisa to know how hard it had been to find the few ingredients on her list, nor to face her disappointment that I had not been totally successful. Even my American dollars had not been able to produce the *piña*, the fresh pineapple that María Luisa's mother longed for.

"Encontraste el jamón?" María Luisa came in from the small patio where she had been hanging the clothes we washed together this morning.

"Si, Marí. I bought two nice pieces of ham from the guy who makes sandwiches in front of the *agro*. He even trimmed the fat off the meat before he weighed it. Look how thick the slices are." Sharing, even in a small way, the deprivations of my friend's life in Cuba had given me a new appreciation for things once taken for granted.

This morning I had arrived at the farmer's market just as it was opening and bought the treasured ham, a couple of onions, a green pepper, and two small bulbs of garlic. Then I went to the dollar store on the corner of 17th and H, where the tourists shopped, and bought a jar of green olives, a bottle of vinegar, and a bag of macaroni for the salad. I longed to buy Lucía a watch with a red plastic band and a face filled with candy that she admired every time we went to that store—but I knew that María Luisa would be upset if I spent money on a toy that would only break.

"María Luisa, este ajo esta totalmente seco, es una basura." María Luisa's mother was taking things out of the bags on the counter. The garlic is all dried up, she told me with an exasperated sigh—it is pure garbage. *"Mami, sientáte,* sit down awhile and rest," María Luisa urged. "You're going to make your blood pressure go up again over the garlic. Don't worry—we'll invent a beautiful salad for the party."

Inventar . . . invent. How many times a day did I hear Cubans use that word now, since things had become so difficult on their island? It captured so much—an acceptance of the limitations, determination to keep going, and a seemingly endless ability to come up with creative solutions. How else did Fords and Chevys built in the 1940s still traverse the streets of the city with their gleaming exteriors and humming engines? There were no parts to be had anywhere in Cuba, but they were invented.

"Elena, when do we have the party, when, when?" Lucía burst through the door—her legs and arms like sticks next to her stocky friend Diana. María Luisa's mother had ignored her daughter's admonitions to rest and was busying herself in the kitchen, putting up the water to boil the macaroni. Everything for the party would be cooked in the morning in case there was a power outage later in the day.

"María Luisa, can you make the *mayonesa* for the salad?" her mother called from the kitchen. They would make the mayonnaise at home rather than pay the $1.89 they charged for a small jar at the dollar store. "Did you get the eggs from Diana's mother?" María Luisa asked. She needed extra eggs to make the mayonnaise, and her neighbor sold them on the black market. "I don't know where she gets them, and I don't ask her," María Luisa had told me. Her mother was one of the very few who still refused to buy from the black-market vendors, but she had relented for Lucía's party. She had bought the eggs from Diana's mother, each one wrapped carefully in the sheets of the daily newspaper that no one bothered to read anymore.

I helped Marí assemble the ingredients for the ensalada. Macaroni, olives, chopped onion and pepper, a little garlic salvaged from the dry cloves I'd purchased, salt, the ham slices chopped finely to distribute the flavor, and home-made mayonnaise. A tiny sparrow flew in through the open shutters and stole a piece of ham. "How I love this kitchen—my little nest among the palm and flamboyan trees!" María Luisa threw her arms in the air and twirled in the middle of her kitchen. She frequently peppered her conversation with dramatic movements and declarations. I knew how hard she and Omar had worked to make this a home, building their furniture from scraps of wood left over from Omar's carpentry workshop. Lucía's colorful crayon drawings covered the old refrigerator and lined the walls. I loved to enter these rooms at the end of a hectic day and feel the peace that they had created here.

"Y la piña?" Marí's mother had reappeared to ask the question I had been dreading all morning. "No pineapple, María del Carmen— not in the agro markets, not in the bodegas, I even looked for canned pineapple in the tourist store. No piña anywhere in Havana today." I could feel her disappointment mist into the air with her heavy sigh. An ensalada fria needs pineapple.

María del Carmen looked so small and old on the couch where she had perched for a moment as I delivered the news about the pineapple. Her hands were chapped and red from the washing, her plastic eyeglasses held together with tape around the hinge that had been broken for a month. Her shoulders slumped with resignation. "Ay, Elena," she began and settled back on the cushions. María Luisa rolled her eyes at me from the kitchen doorway. I knew that I was about to hear another story about the way things were in the good old days, when her Uncle Ray used to pile the whole family in the back of his truck and take them to the beach at Guardalavaca. Her story would be filled with memories of the flavor and aroma of the food they prepared for the trip—the pig roasted over an open fire, the black beans rich with garlic and *vino seco*, the yellow rice taken right off the stove to the beach. And Tío Ray handing out sandy slices of watermelon and pineapple—the cousins laughing as the sweet juice trickled down their arms and then running, running to the sea.

María del Carmen's nostalgia was for a time when the revolution was young and the air was full of hope. She'd hidden *guerrilleros* in her home during the fighting and then gone to the mountains herself during the literacy campaign—hiking the trails, sleeping in rough shelters, teaching the peasants to read. When she arrived in Havana, her life was full of new and undreamed-of luxury—an apartment that belonged to her, a Russian refrigerator awarded for being an outstanding worker, a university education for her daughters, a doctor who came to her home once a week to check her blood pressure, tins of smoked fish and ham on her shelves.

María Luisa's mother could not reconcile herself to the scarcity and hardship they were facing each day. She felt betrayed by the whispered offerings of the black-market sellers and the beckoning gaze of the gaudy prostitutes strolling beside the seawall each night. She felt betrayed by the neighbors whose satellite dish brought TV shows from Miami, by María Luisa's young coworker in the theater group who confided his plan to leave for Mexico, by the endless and empty promises of the bureaucrats. She felt that betrayal like hot, acid bile that rose up in her throat because there was no pineapple for the salad for her granddaughter's birthday. I could see it on her face. There was nothing I could say.

I returned to the kitchen to help María Luisa finish the salad. She molded it into a clown's face that would amuse Lucía and her friends, with two olives for eyes and one of the red *pimientos* for a mouth. Omar would arrive soon, I hoped, with the cake. He probably had to wait in a long line—or maybe they had run out of cakes. That happened sometimes.

No matter. I knew my friend María Luisa would invent this birthday party for her daughter out of thin air if she had to—with condoms blown up for balloons, with whatever Omar could bring back from the bakery, with an ensalada fria in the shape of a clown.

"*Mamita,* come and see what I have done with the salad. How Lucía will laugh when she sees it. Mamita, *venga*—come here and see!"

But María Luisa's mother didn't answer her call and she didn't come to see the clown face. She had returned to the patio and was slowly hanging the towels that we had washed that morning, one by one, on the line.

*Maria Luisa's home became a refuge for me and I was thrilled
to be named Lucia's honorary "tia."*

CHAPTER TWELVE

LIFE ON THE MARGINS

The secret I kept for two years during Clarence's illness still held so much power that, for years after his death, when someone innocently asked "How did your husband die?" my breath caught in my chest and the words stuck in my throat. I found myself carefully taking the measure of the person who would receive the information. Why did they ask? How would they judge me once they knew? What unspoken questions would I see in their eyes?

"I don't want everyone to see me as your husband who has AIDS," Clarence had said when we first discussed how to share information about his illness. "I want them to know me first as a person, not as a disease, or a label." I had thought it a bit ironic that he could rise in front of a group at nightly Narcotics Anonymous (NA) meetings and declare, "My name is Clarence and I'm an addict," but not feel comfortable having me tell my colleagues at work what we were going through. But, as he had repeatedly pointed out, "I'm the one living with this virus," so I had swallowed my own need to unburden myself. I had gone to work each day. I had kept the secret.

Perhaps it was this personal experience with the power of secrets that had propelled me to look for Roberto in his room in the AIDS sanatorium one rainy afternoon in August, and to ask the questions that would unlock the secret he had been keeping from me.

The group had taken a few days off between sessions, and it had been great to see everyone together, fresh and eager to begin again. The members of the AIDS Prevention Group, all residents of the sanatorium, were preparing to go out to Havana neighborhoods to teach others about how to prevent HIV infection. And they were going to "*dar la cara al publico*" (literally give their face to the public)—to tell their personal stories in public for the first time. I had told my own story at meetings and conferences in the US and understood the value of this kind of testimony, how it could break down walls of suspicion and fear. But this would be a new activity for members of the Prevention Group. In my workshop session, they would have a chance to practice in a safe space.

The night before the workshop, in my rented room in Havana, I had perched cross-legged on my bed, squinting in the dim light from the bare bulb on my ceiling and written out some questions on folded slips of paper. It had taken me a while to translate the questions into my still-awkward Spanish, and I had read them aloud to my landlady, Ruki, to make sure that they made sense. *Como supiste del diagnostico?* How did you learn of your diagnosis? *Y cuales fueron tus sentimientos?* How did you feel? Have you told others about your diagnosis? How did they react? Have you ever been really sick? Do you ever think about dying? *En suicidiste?* About suicide?

We sat in a circle on hard plastic chairs borrowed from the dining hall. I asked for volunteers to take a turn at answering a question drawn from a baseball cap. Alejandro was with us that day and volunteered to go first. He drew out the question, "How did you first find out about your diagnosis and how did you feel?" He stood before the group and spoke in a strong, clear voice, vividly conveying the horror of being told by military personnel, "You have AIDS, you will probably die soon," before being whisked away to the hospital. Heads were nodding around the room as he spoke. There were others who remembered those early harsh days of Cuba's AIDS program.

The cap made its way around the circle to Hermes. "I'm nervous," he had said, fishing around for a slip of paper. He frowned a bit as he read his question and pushed his thick dark hair away from his eyes. "Can I stay sitting?" he had asked with a little laugh. "My question is, 'Have you ever thought about dying,'" Hermes went on, his deep voice gathering strength as he spoke. "My images of this illness were from pictures I saw on TV of people very deteriorated and sick. That's what stayed in my mind. I had the feeling that my life was over, as if I had no future. So I left my job and for almost a year I just waited for the end."

As the cap continued around the circle, people told their stories with tears and humor, and everyone listened intently. Even the arrival of our midmorning snack of papaya juice and cheese sandwiches failed to disrupt the silent attention the group focused on each speaker.

Roberto was one of the newest members of the group and had drawn the last question from the cap. We waited for his answer. It was almost time for lunch.

"*No quiero responder,*" he said in a trembling voice. "I don't feel comfortable answering the question." All eyes were trained on Roberto. This was unexpected. I hoped my Spanish would carry me through.

"*Está bien, Roberto.* That's fine," I assured him. "It's okay to say that you'd rather not answer a question."

And to the group: "Sometimes people ask very personal things that you won't want to talk about. You have a right to decline, but try to be respectful."

Then we stopped for lunch and an extended afternoon break to allow people to collect their weekly food ration.

Roberto did not return to the workshop that afternoon or the next day. The question he had picked from the cap, left folded and unanswered on his chair, was "What prevention message can you pass on to others based on your own personal experience?"

We were all worried about Roberto and concerned that he had not returned to the training program, so several days later I went in search of him. There were several *barrios* or neighborhoods within the sanatorium and, like housing in the outside community, it was a combination of seniority, luck, and persistence that seemed to determine where one ended up. The best neighborhood, where Caridad lived, consisted of one- and two-family homes surrounded by gardens. Roberto lived in a large building, much like a college dorm, in an area that housed many of the sanatorium's newer and younger residents. A drafting table covered with markers, rulers, and cardboard dominated his simple room. Roberto was the artist of the group and was employed at the sanatorium designing posters, signs, and announcements. He was a tall man with strong features and a large handlebar mustache. He wore his black hair long, just brushing the top of his shirt collar, and his appearance, like his room, was neat and orderly.

Roberto took a seat on the edge of his bed and motioned me to a wooden bench under the window. A steady rain beat against the metal louvers which were open to allow a faint breeze to cool the room. I shrugged off my backpack and laid it on the bench beside me. A small gray-striped kitten batted at my legs and leapt at Roberto's hands, always in motion, as he spoke. It was rare to see a pet kitten in Cuba during these times when food was so hard to come by—and there was always a joke or two circulating that alluded to their eventual consumption in some kind of stew.

A group of young guys had gathered right outside the room and were trading noisy insults, so Roberto got up to close the door. The kitten retreated under the bed for the moment, and Roberto leaned toward me speaking slowly and quietly. "I want you to understand why I couldn't answer the question at the workshop, Elena," he began. "It is not an easy thing to explain."

Roberto walked to the wooden dresser in a corner of the room, picked up a framed photo and handed it to me. Two little girls, about a year apart in age, dressed in their blue school uniforms with ribbons in their hair, looked seriously out at me from the photo. "My daughters," he said. "I was married. I had my two beautiful daughters. I was working. Then everything began to fall apart."

Roberto sat next to me on the bench as he described a year in which his marriage ended and he had to move out of his apartment. Then he lost his job. With no place to go and no real support from his family, he became very depressed. "I had an emotional breakdown, Elena. I just couldn't pull my life together," he went on, pacing between the dresser and the bed. "The only one who really cared about me, whom I felt close to, was my sister. And she was living here. She had HIV. I saw her life here; she had a lot of support, and she was living well."

Roberto paused for a moment, rocking on his heels, covering his eyes with his hand.

"I decided I wanted to be here with her." He stopped in front of me, his arms loose at his sides. I kept my eyes on his face, encouraging him to go on.

"So I bought blood from someone who was infected with the virus, contaminated blood, and injected myself with it."

I shifted uncomfortably on the hard wooden bench, trying to take in what Roberto was saying. I had a million questions, but felt that to ask even one would be an intrusion. Roberto's story was almost beyond my comprehension. To feel so desperate and alone in the world that the only solution was to inject oneself with a deadly virus—how could I begin to understand that?

Finally I ventured a gently probing question. "Wasn't there any other way for you to get help at that time?" I asked. "Oh yes," he replied, "there were other ways, but I wasn't thinking, I wasn't struggling in the way that I should have. I tried a desperate measure and after I did, I saw that I had made a terrible mistake. But it was too late."

Roberto sat on the edge of the bed, exhausted from the effort of explaining himself to me. But there was one more thing he wanted me to know.

"Most of the other people here who have injected themselves," he told me, "they are prostitutes, promiscuous, drug addicts. They have led *una vida disorganizada*, a very disorganized life." Roberto pulled himself off the bed and strode to the window as if to emphasize the importance of his next words. "I am the only such case in the entire sanatorium who did not have that kind of life."

By that time, I had come to understand that the term "una vida disorganizada" was a catchphrase for every type of marginalized behavior in Cuba. In the sanatorium, life seemed relatively free of the expectations that shaped Cuban life on the outside—the high value placed on being a productive, contributing member of a collective society seemed tempered on the leafy paths of Los Cocos. Gay couples lived openly together, something that was still challenging on the outside; transvestites were free to dress in any way they chose; punk rockers flaunted their antiauthoritarian styles without fear of harassment or censure. The virus somehow erased the need to conform.

But there was a price to pay for this relative freedom. In Roberto's case, because of his history of self-infection, he had been required to undergo two years of evaluation before he could be judged confiable or trustworthy and be able to leave the sanatorium for good. In the meantime, he was allowed to leave on weekend passes to visit his daughters, but only with an acompañante, a health worker who served as a chaperone. Roberto described in humorous detail the difficulties of having a guardian always with you—particularly in light of Cuba's economic woes.

"If I want to spend the whole day sitting on the Malecón looking at the waves hit the shore, and I have nothing to eat, then he has to spend the day on the Malecón not eating. I have to think of myself and of him when I plan my weekend." The acompañante evaluated

Roberto's conduct on these weekend visits and then reported back to his evaluation committee at the sanatorium.

The rain was beginning to let up, and it was nearly time for me to catch the bus back to Havana. Roberto opened the door to his room and handed me my backpack. He paused for a moment in the open doorway. "I get counseling here, Elena. The psychologists help me a lot, and the group supports me. I am comfortable here. But it is not easy."

Roberto's story stayed in my mind for weeks after we spoke. I kept turning it around and around, trying to get a handle on it, to feel what he must have been going through. I knew that Roberto's was not the only case of infection acquired through self-injection of blood contaminated with HIV. I had read a story in *The New York Times Magazine* some years back which claimed that young Cuban rockers were buying contaminated blood on the black market or getting it from friends and injecting themselves so that they could live in the sanatorium. They were harassed, fined, sometimes beaten up or jailed for their antisocial attitudes and actions, and wanted to escape to the easier life they had heard about—better food, better housing, no need to work or go to school. Perhaps they believed that they could get the virus without getting sick or that there would soon be a cure.

The Ministry of Health officials I talked to acknowledged that some people had indeed been infected by self-injection, but it was hard to get anyone to put a number on it. The official number I was given was nine, but some doctors and patients I spoke with at the sanatorium claimed personal knowledge of many more than that.

If I had never met Roberto and heard his story, the Cuban phenomenon of self-infection with HIV would have remained yet another aspect of this very different culture that puzzled me. There was no way for me to know if everything that Roberto told me was true. Maybe there had been other reasons for his action. But I found myself returning over and over to his act of desperation. Was there anything in my own experience I could use to understand what had moved him to do what he did?

During the first years of my life with Clarence, he was trying to kick a heroin habit that had started years earlier when he first got back from Vietnam. He had been in and out of rehab. He'd do well for a while, but then would relapse and start the cycle all over again.

Clarence didn't fit my preconceived ideas about what a "drug addict" or "junkie" would look or act like. He held a steady job in the post office and was a shop steward in his union. He took his daughter to the movies or on bike rides when she visited on the weekends. His Marine Corps training sent him out into the world each day with spit-shined shoes and a sharp crease in his pants. Even his mother refused to believe he was using drugs after he finally hit bottom and called her from a VA hospital. "I guess he musta been, cause he says he was, but I just don't see it, I just don't," she had told me at the time.

I was working as a visiting nurse by then, and already AIDS was starting to enter my world. Robin, a little boy I took care of in Washington Heights, greeted me with a smile that grew weaker each day. His thin legs were not strong enough to carry him very far anymore, and he spent the day watching cartoons on the couch. I was struck by his emaciated face, pale dry skin, and brittle coppery hair. It was a look I had not seen before up close, but would grow so used to as time went on that I would see someone with a similar look on the street and think, *I wonder if he has AIDS.*

Clarence worked the night shift at the post office. When his shift ended, at about five in the morning, he would often head into New York, to the Lower East Side, to cop some drugs. At that point he wasn't using drugs to get high but just to keep from going into withdrawal, from feeling sick. He told me later that he didn't keep his own "works" (needles and syringes) in our apartment because he wanted his drug life and family life to be completely separate. So he went to shooting galleries to get a fix and then came home and went to sleep. On some level, I must have known when he was using, but like Clarence's mom, I chose not to see. By the time I got home in the afternoon, he was up doing chores around the house, a little grumpy maybe, but just a regular guy, tired from working the night shift.

Was Clarence's nightly trip into a shooting gallery on the Lower East Side, where he shared a needle with a total stranger to shoot drugs into his vein, so different from Roberto's desperate act of self-destruction?

Later, when AIDS had come closer still, when friends from Clarence's Narcotics Anonymous (NA) program got sick and we didn't see them anymore, Clarence convinced himself that he had stopped using drugs just in time, that he had "dodged the bullet," as he put it then. By that time I knew better. I knew how long the virus could lie in wait undetected.

"I'm not gonna go lookin' for trouble, babe," Clarence told me when I suggested maybe he should get tested. "If trouble wants to find me, it will." When I suggested that maybe we should start using condoms, he was hurt and angry. "Are you trying to tell me you think I'm sick? You gotta have a more positive attitude, babe." So I dropped it, let it go, never brought it up again. I worried silently, lying beside Clarence in the night, but I never said another word. I remembered Clarence's statement about denial not being just a river in Egypt. Clarence and I were both deep in denial.

When I think about that time in my life now, I am stunned, embarrassed at my lack of self-protection. What was I thinking? How could I have exposed myself like that? I was a professional. I counseled people about safe sex and HIV prevention all day long. I remembered one patient in particular who had shaken my professional detachment, though I didn't realize it at the time.

Late one afternoon, Keisha shuffled into the tiny counseling room at the pediatric AIDS program where I worked as a nurse. It was the end of a very long day in the clinic. I knew that Dr. Arry had just informed her that she was infected with the HIV virus. It was my job to counsel her about safer sex and taking care of herself.

Keisha's lightly freckled brown face and neat cornrows clipped with pink plastic barrettes went with her age—just fourteen. But her eyes had the weary, seen-it-all look of a much older woman. She plopped down in the chair opposite me, cracking her gum, studying the posters encouraging condom use on the wall.

"Hey Keisha," I said, trying to make eye contact. "I know you just got some news from the doctor and I'd like to hear how you are feeling about it."

"It's no big thing," Keisha replied, still gazing everywhere but in my direction. "I was kinda expecting it, I guess. I just kinda figured I would get it sooner or later."

I was glad that Keisha was not looking at me as I struggled to compose my face after hearing this statement. She just popped it out into the air between us with no visible emotion and let it lie there. I was unsure about how to proceed.

"Do you have family or friends that have the virus, Keisha?" I needed a little more information to be able to process this.

"My cousin and my baby's daddy," she spoke the words flatly with no inflection. "Well, me and my friends, we just figure we're all gonna get the virus. If not that, then the drugs will get us, or the gangs. I just don't think I'm gonna be around to a ripe old age."

I knew what Keisha's world looked like. As a nurse I had trudged the hilly streets of Washington Heights in New York City visiting young Dominican women who were raising their kids in one room of someone else's apartment—with extension cords fueling the electric hotplates where they cooked the family meals. I had walked through the worn lobbies of once-beautiful Art Deco apartment buildings, skirting jittery lines of young men waiting to score coke or smack. I had driven through the burnt-out streets of Newark, past acres of vacant lots left from riots that had occurred thirty years earlier, and crossed the trash-littered, broken pavement of public housing projects to climb dark, urine-soaked stairs to the tired apartments where young girls like Keisha lived.

I went through the motions with Keisha that day—my usual rap about keeping herself healthy, making sure she didn't give the virus to anyone else. She slipped the condoms I gave her into the back pocket of her jeans along with the slip of paper that noted her next appointment in a month. I didn't expect to ever see her again, and I never did.

Roberto, Keisha, Clarence, I—we were worlds apart, weren't we? Loving Clarence had exposed me to a kind of judgment I had been aware of before, but not had to face personally. Everywhere we went, people made assumptions about us. When we got on the checkout line at the supermarket, the clerk separated our food into two orders. When I took him to the ER, the nurses asked if I was his social worker. One day we were waiting together at his doctor's office. Clarence had been steadily losing weight despite all the smothered pork chops and fried chicken his mother cooked up. The doctor's regular secretary was out, and a temp was in her place at the front desk. Dr. Fields was running late. We were thumbing through magazines when Susan, the wife of a friend from Clarence's NA program, came into the waiting room with her new baby. She was also a patient of Dr. Fields. We had visited them when the baby was born, but he was now a chubby, alert three-month-old. Clarence grinned and held out his arms for the baby. Just then the nurse called him into the exam room. I went back to my magazines. Later that day, Susan called to tell us that the temporary clerk had taken her aside after Clarence went in to see the doctor. "I wouldn't let him hold your baby, dear," the clerk had told her. "He has AIDS, you know."

I was married to a black Vietnam vet who was a recovering drug addict living with AIDS. What did this mean about me? At work I winced when I heard well-meaning volunteers talk about the "innocent victims" of this epidemic—the babies and children, the hemophiliacs. This implied that there were guilty ones. But even among the "guilty" there was a hierarchy of sin. Women who were unknowingly infected by their sexual partners were innocent, but if they chose to get pregnant in spite of the risks of passing on the virus to their baby, they joined the ranks of the guilty. Gay men were bad, but at least they only put each other at risk. Guiltiest of all, lowest on this weird totem pole of accusation and blame, were the junkies. They thought of nothing but getting high—and they lived among us, they had sex with us, they placed our lives in danger.

A similar hierarchy of blame existed in Cuba. It took me a while to understand it. The dividing line seemed to be between those who were viewed as "productive" members of Cuban society and those who were hanging out on the margins, who refused to contribute. The first Cubans infected with HIV had been people who traveled out of the country—diplomats, artists, and soldiers, all respected for their role in Cuban society. The fact that they probably acquired the infection through illicit sexual liaisons did not seem to matter much. Sexuality in Cuba was openly expressed, and affairs were common and tolerated, for both husbands and wives.

Homosexuality was another matter. There had been moments of intense political repression of homosexuals when they weren't allowed to join the Communist Party or serve as teachers. In fact, in the first years after the revolution, camps had been set up in the countryside, called UMAP or Military Units to Help Production. This program forced thousands of members of religious organizations, homosexuals, intellectuals and artists whose support for the revolution was questioned, as well as those deemed "anti-social," into agricultural labor camps. UMAP began in November of 1965 and was ended in July of 1968 after Fidel Castro personally visited one of the camps, and the Cuban government later acknowledged that the program had been a mistake.

But those gay men, like my friends Hermes and Alejandro in the sanatorium, who were educated and *responsable*, were admired. Drag queens, transvestites, rockers, the young girls who hung out in front of the tourist hotels looking to befriend an *extranjero*—these were the *gente marginada*, the marginalized people that the psychologists at the sanatorium often talked about.

But even life on the margins in Cuba puzzled me. I had to look through a different lens to see it. In New York, on my way to work each day, I passed a legless man sitting on a filthy piece of cardboard. "Homeless Vet. I have AIDS. Please Help Me," his hand-lettered sign implored. On my walk down Broadway to the subway, I dodged people weaving across the sidewalk in conversation with themselves. That's what life on the margins looked like to me back home, but I had trouble recognizing it in Cuba, on the quiet leafy paths of the sanatorium.

Was it that socialist Cuba provided a true "safety net" so that no one was lost? Roberto had created the circumstances that led to his infection, but was cared for and supported in a residential community where he received free shelter, food, counseling, and healthcare, and was encouraged to work as an artist and paid a salary. In Havana, I had visited a neighborhood close to where I was living called *El Fangüito* (the Little Muddy)—a poor barrio on the banks of the Rio Almendares dotted with shanty homes built of scrap lumber and tin. The local family doctor had done a lot of outreach in the community and won the trust of a group of young girls who were hanging out at tourist hotels and discos, trading sex with foreigners for material goods. The Cubans called these young girls *jineteras*, which literally meant female jockeys, refraining from labeling them prostitutes. And though their activities were frowned on, most lived at home and received regular, free health care at the neighborhood clinic run by the family doctor. According to her, these young girls came looking for information about STDs and AIDS and were eager to find out how to protect themselves.

Tanya had lived the life of a jinetera before entering the sanatorium. She strolled slowly into the dining hall on the third day of the training course, her pink plastic sandals *slap-slapping* on the tiles to announce her late entrance. Tanya's hair was cut to within an inch of her scalp and bleached platinum blonde. A faded tattoo of a pierced heart was visible above the upper edge of her tube top, and a peace sign was inked onto her left arm. Her cutoff denim shorts barely scraped the tops of her thighs. She selected an empty chair and sat down with a nervous laugh. "I'm Tanya, the poet," she stated in a flat voice. "I'm here."

The rest of the Prevention Group seemed wary of Tanya. She came and went during the months that we conducted the workshop, but was never invited to speak in public. Often she seemed deliberately provocative, throwing out a question or a comment to see what the reaction would be.

"Why do we try to tell other people what to do with their lives?" she asked one day. "Nobody gives up what they like. If they like sex, they don't give it up." I shifted in my seat, thinking of my own flawed effort at practicing safer sex with Clarence.

Occasionally she showed up with a poem to read to the group. Her poems were serious and lyrical, with titles like *"Muerte"* (Death) and *"Muerte II," "Final,"* and *"Entierro"* (Burial).

On March 8th, International Women's Day, which was celebrated as a national holiday in Cuba, she brought a more uplifting poem and read it aloud.

"La mujer, con gallardia rebrevero su concienca,
con infinita paciencia aunque viva en agonia . . ."

I didn't understand every word. Something about a woman who lives with infinite patience though she lives in agony. The ending of the poem was easier for me.

"A ti, mujer positiva,
te quiero felicitar y mi saludo brindar
porque tu eres mi amiga."

I toast to you, positive woman, the poem's ending declares, in a play on words on "positive," *because you are my friend.*

The language she used in her poetry was sophisticated, but in real life Tanya was often impish and silly. I was intrigued and wanted to know more about her. One day we sat down to talk and she told me about her life as a *friki.*

We sat on an old wooden bench in the shade on the path to the Administration Building to have our conversation. Tanya had brought her lunch with her in a plastic container, which she held in her lap while we talked. Her narration was punctuated by spells of coughing, and her voice was breathy as if speaking took too much energy. "I was really sick last year," she told me. "I had pneumonia twice."

Tanya was thirty-three when I met her and had been living in the sanatorium for eight years. Her nine-year-old daughter, Yaimert, lived in Havana with Tanya's mother. Cuba's AIDS policy had recently changed to make living in the sanatorium voluntary.

"Do you think you will leave?" I asked Tanya.

"I'm doing well here," she said. "I'm not planning to leave the sanatorium. I'm scared that if I leave something may happen to me. I'll get sick. I'm not adapted to the street after so much time in here."

"Tell me about your poetry, Tanya." I wrote poetry as a young girl and had recently begun to write again. I was curious about how Tanya got started.

"I wrote poems from the time I was young, about nine years old. First I would write a poem and then throw it away," she began, and then went on to tell me about the *Montaña Magia*, a literary workshop she was introduced to when she first got to the sanatorium. What had been a hobby before now defined her life.

"When I was sixteen, seventeen years old, I started having a lot of boyfriends," Tanya went on. "I was always looking for someone with tastes like mine, someone I would be compatible with."

In the early 1980s in Cuba, a group of young people called *frikis* had created a counterculture that combined aspects of the hippie and rocker culture. Tanya had been attracted to the sexual freedom of the group, but even more to the "freedom of thought," as she described it. "They read a lot—Kafka, Walt Whitman, all those people who are revolutionaries. It was like a rebirth of ideas for me."

The friki group that Tanya hung out with was defined by their appearance. The girls wore very tight pants, lots of bracelets and earrings, punk hairdos. The boys wore their hair long. They lived a nocturnal life, sleeping wherever they ended up—at bus stops, under bridges, sometimes in fields in the country. Tanya began to read the Bible and to wear a cross.

"How did your family react to all of this, Tanya?" I asked as she opened her lunch container and began to nibble on a sandwich.

"They didn't like it. They didn't like that I wore a cross because Christianity was not viewed in a good light. They didn't understand that I got interesting ideas from the Bible and I applied them in my own way to my world." I found it amusing that the thing about her lifestyle that her family was most concerned about was her apparent attraction to Christianity!

"I was a hippie myself once," I told Tanya. "In the sixties, in San

Francisco. I lived in a van that was painted all different colors and traveled around the country for a few months." We had a good laugh then. Tanya put down her sandwich and looked me up and down with new interest—this public-health teacher from the States confessing her checkered past. "My parents weren't too happy about it either."

I was skirting the issue I really wanted to ask about, not knowing how to bring it up. How could I ask her if she had been a jinetera, a prostitute? I suspected that many of the mothers of kids I took care of in the clinic had traded sex for drugs—and ultimately for the virus— but I had never spoken with them about it.

"My daughter comes here to visit me," Tanya said, breaking into my reflection. "I explain to her what kind of place this is and why I am here, the illness I have. She takes care of me. She really understands me."

Finally I took a chance. "Tanya, you once told me that you were a jinetera. Do you feel like talking about that now?"

"I had pretty good luck with that," Tanya stated in that flat voice I was growing accustomed to, so matter of fact and seemingly devoid of feeling. "Cars stopped for me. They took me places. They bought me things. But it wasn't really my way of life. I didn't really care about the money."

Tanya packed up the remains of her lunch and stood up, letting me know our conversation was coming to an end. "I'm hoping for a vaccine, for a cure. But if no cure appears, well, I'd like to last five or six more years."

And then, from over her shoulder as she walked away, her sandals slapping on the concrete pathway—she threw one last disconnected provocative question my way. "What will you take with you when you die, Elena? Money? I don't think so. You'll take your feelings, no?"

When I had first arrived in Cuba at the beginning of my fieldwork project, I compared the experience of understanding this complex culture to that of eating an artichoke—peeling away the layers of leaves. As soon as I peeled away one layer, another appeared. My conversations with Roberto and Tanya had helped me peel one more layer.

I saw Roberto one more time as I was preparing to wrap up my work and leave Cuba to go home. We sat on the grass under a mango tree in a quiet corner of the courtyard outside his building, and he caught me up on his life. He was hopeful that he might be able to get back together with his wife. They had begun seeing each other during his weekend visits. His sister had a new boyfriend he didn't get along with, and it was putting a strain on their close relationship.

"There's one more question I've wanted to ask you, Roberto." He smiled broadly, smoothing his moustache and flashing his teeth.

"Don't you ever get tired of asking questions?"

"Well, I wanted to know—if you were going to answer the question you picked out of the cap that day in the workshop, what would you say right now, today? *Is* there an AIDS prevention message you can pass on to others?"

Roberto looked down for a moment, ruffling the grass with his fingers.

"It is hard, Elena," he said, "to stand up and say, 'I did this to myself.' A lot of people feel I shouldn't be involved in prevention work, but I know I do have something to teach others."

And then Roberto placed his hand on my shoulder as he rose from the grass and quoted José Martí, the hero of Cuba's war of independence from Spain: "'Man doesn't learn from the times he falls down,'" Roberto said, "'but from the times he picks himself up.' Martí said that, and that's what I believe, Elena, that's what I hope."

*Roberto in a playful moment with a kitten
in his room at the sanatorium.*

Tanya and I in conversation about poetry and life.

CHAPTER THIRTEEN

TELLING OUR STORIES

The group met after lunch in the workers' cafeteria at the sanatorium, scraping the floor with our hard metal chairs as we gathered them in a circle, and straining to be heard over the hum of the ancient air conditioner and the clinking of dishes being washed in the kitchen. We'd been meeting several days a week for more than two months and going through an intense curriculum of knowledge and practice—about the virus, prevention methods, and educational strategies.

That afternoon we were eight—six members of the peer education group, a Cuban health educator who had joined the session, and I. I was teaching a session I called "Telling Our Stories," the second part of a workshop we had designed to help the members of the group gain the confidence to speak about their personal experiences.

I looked around the circle at the small group I had grown so close to. Most were already aware that that my husband, Clarence, had died of AIDS in 1990, but now I would reveal more. I would tell my own story to the group, as I had many times before in meetings and conferences in the US.

"I usually start at the beginning," I began slowly, standing in the middle of the circle, consulting the notes I had worked on the night before, curled up on my bed at Ruki's, writing them out in Spanish on large pink and blue colored index cards.

"We probably all remember the moment when our lives changed." I went on. "Clarence was diagnosed in 1988 and our world turned upside down. There weren't many medications then to stop the disease from getting worse. Soon after Clarence got sick, I started working in a pediatric AIDS clinic in Newark, so I was immersed in AIDS, at work and at home. After a hard day in the clinic, I went home to take care of Clarence. When he kept me up at night with a constant dry cough, I wondered if it was a symptom of something worse than just a cold. The stigma of having AIDS was so intense then. Clarence's illness was a secret I shared only with my family and a few close friends. I felt so alone. I was on a rollercoaster of hope and fear."

The room grew quiet as I continued. A few of the cafeteria workers had gathered around the edges of our circle, and the afternoon snack of cheese and bread lay untouched on the rusty metal table behind me. Memories of that time in my life, six years earlier, flashed through my mind as I lost myself in the telling, pausing only to find the right Spanish word to describe my feelings.

"How did you cope after Clarence died, Elena?" Caridad motioned me to sit in the chair next to her. Like me, Caridad was a young widow. Like me, she had watched helplessly as her husband Orlando's vitality and strength was drained by his battle with AIDS. Like me, she had cared for him in the last months of his life and then had been left to carry on alone when he died, just eight months earlier. Orlando had been a soldier in Cuba's war against apartheid forces in Angola, a hero who returned home to parades and honors only to be felled by a microscopic virus.

Clarence too had been a veteran—of the Vietnam War, a wounded warrior battling heroin addiction. By the time we met, he was finding his way to recovery, but not soon enough to save him from AIDS. Caridad and I had felt the painful bond of our shared experience from the moment we met, but we were also aware of the differences in our stories. She had been left to cope with her own infection—a fate I had somehow escaped.

"What is this picture, Elena?" Hermes's deep baritone voice broke through the group's silence. A photograph of the AIDS Quilt panels I had created for Clarence was making its way around the circle.

"This is a picture of the AIDS Quilt"—I searched for the word in Spanish and settled for *colcha*, though that meant blanket and wasn't exactly right. "Have you heard about it?" Heads shook across the circle. No one had. "It's a huge memorial for all the people who have died of AIDS in the US—a way of remembering and honoring them," I explained. "Clarence's family and I made four quilt panels for him, and then they were sewn together with all of these other ones." The photo was back in my hands now and I pointed to all the panels stitched together, covering the entire National Mall, all the way to the Washington Monument. In the photo I was kneeling on the grass and patting the fabric beside me. I remembered that day so well.

"*Ay, que bella,*" Caridad spoke in a voice so soft we all leaned forward in our chairs to hear her. "It's beautiful, Elena. I would love to make something like this for Orlando."

"Wow! *Tremendo idea!*" Alejandro spoke up next. "Maybe we can make a panel for the tenth anniversary of the sanatorium to honor the members of the group who are no longer with us. There will be a big celebration in April. We have no memorials here in Cuba for our *compañeros* who have died of AIDS. Do you think we could start with just one panel?"

I put aside my outline for the rest of the workshop as ideas flew around the room. By the end of the afternoon we had a plan. People would begin to collect scraps of fabric and materials to decorate the panel. My daughter, Angelica, was coming down to visit me and I would ask her to bring some lengths of plain fabric, thread, and other things that were hard to come by in Cuba. The group would meet every week to work on the project.

"I have never visited Clarence's grave since the day his coffin was lowered into it," I told the group as we folded the chairs and stacked them along the wall at the end of our meeting, "but I have been to see the AIDS quilt many times—in Washington, DC, in Newark, New Jersey, in New York City. It's truly a living memorial—so many lives have been joined into one by the quilt. I'm so glad I was able to share it with you."

This photo of Clarence's quilt panels served as a catalyst for Proyecto Memorias, the Cuban AIDS quilt.

CHAPTER FOURTEEN

MOTHER AND CHILD REUNION

One weekend, shortly after we began talking about the quilt project, Caridad invited me along on a visit to see her only child, her son José, in Santa Cruz del Norte. They had been separated for months at a time when she tested positive for HIV and was sent to live in the sanatorium. She tried to see him as often as she could. Carnota, one of the psychologists at the sanatorium, had offered to drive. "Maybe you could even interview José about our family's experience," Cari had suggested. I had jumped at the chance to get out of the city for the day and to meet her beloved son.

The ride was noisy, bumpy, and long in Carnota's twenty-year-old, Russian-made Lada. Even in the front seat of the car, I felt every pothole as he navigated through road construction and detours. One detour took us through the industrial section of the port where containers were waiting to be loaded onto ships—one from Venezuela and another from Greece. A large smokestack sent flames and thick black smoke into the air. The coarse sand by the side of the road was stained with oil, and the hot air that assaulted us through the open windows of the un–air-conditioned car was thick with the smell of diesel fuel. I was surprised at how much renewal activity was going on in the old part of the city—and that Carnota paid a toll to travel through the tunnel that crossed Havana Bay. This was new; tolls and a variety of taxes had been instituted in the early 1990s to pull Cuba out of her economic crisis.

Cari sat in the back, happy to be visiting her only child who had moved to this small fishing town north of Havana several months earlier. In her lap she cradled a bag containing three baby pigeons she was bringing to José, who raised them as a hobby. Every once in a while, one of the birds emitted a high-pitched squeal and thrashed around in the bag. Once Cari insisted we pull over as she was sure that a pigeon had died. A little fresh air revived the bird (and us), and we continued on our journey.

On the outskirts of Havana, I glimpsed a large billboard displaying the strongest political slogan I had seen on this trip. *BLOQUEO YANQUI,* it announced in bold red letters, *GENOCIDIA CONTRA CUBA.* The Yankee blockade. Genocide against Cuba. Carnota slowed down so I could take a photo. *"Un poco fuerte,"* he muttered under his breath. A little strong. But I was aware more than ever of the damaging effects of U.S. policy.

We traveled the fifty-two kilometers to Santa Cruz without mishap. The highway hugged the coast most of the way. Fifty- and sixty-year-old Fords and Chevys shared the road with battered diesel trucks loaded up with goods being transported out of the capital. It seemed to me that there was more traffic moving on the roads now than when I had visited three years ago, but when I voiced this observation, it was met with a shrug, as if these small changes had no real impact on daily life in Cuba.

We finally arrived at the turnoff for Santa Cruz del Norte and headed off in search of José. Caridad guided us to a small cement house just off the main highway. José met us at the car and relieved his mother of the bag of pigeons. I had not seen him for nine years— not since he was a young boy playing in the yard and waiting for his father, Orlando, to finish a meeting. He had grown into a brawny, muscled, handsome young man. In the broad grin that José flashed me, I could see Orlando.

We settled into wooden rockers in the dark front room of the house, sipping on glasses of fresh cold mango juice. The house belonged to the mother of a boarding school pal of José's. Cari exchanged warm greetings with family members who drifted into the living room to see her. "They were like a second family to my son during the first years that Orlando and I were in the AIDS sanatorium," she told me. "He stayed here on weekends and school vacations. They were the only people outside of our family who really knew what was going on."

José had moved to Santa Cruz several months earlier after he got married. He and his young wife lived with her parents, but he hung out in the home of his boyhood friend during the day while she was at work. José hadn't found work yet, but he was looking. Santa Cruz was home to several other industries besides fishing. There was a large thermoelectric plant, the Camilo Cienfuegos sugar cane factory, a soda bottling operation, and a factory that produced boxes from pressed wood made from sugar cane. José really wanted to work in one of the Canadian-owned hotels in the area, where tips in dollars and monthly "goody" bags containing shampoo, soap, and other personal hygiene products augmented the meager salaries. His wife had recently started working as a hotel housekeeper, but he had not yet been so lucky.

A large rum factory that produced Havana Club was also located nearby, and José and Carnota went off in search of cheap rum, TuKola (Cuba's version of Coca Cola), and fish. If they were successful, the Lada would be loaded for our return trip to Havana. In the early 1990s, I still encountered many Cubans who adamantly refused to buy on the black market and condemned those who did as undermining the revolution. But by 1996, stealing from state-owned enterprises was rampant, and almost everyone seemed to take advantage of the available products. Black-market offerings varied from place to place, based on whatever was being produced in the area. When I mentioned with amusement to a friend the white cement seller I'd met one evening in Havana, he knew exactly who I was talking about— the cement seller was apparently a well-known businessman in the neighborhood. In moments of cynical musing at this phenomenon, I imagined writing a travel guide to Cuba that would be based on the black-market products that were available in each location. *In lovely Santa Cruz del Norte*, my guidebook might read, *look for vendors offering the finest Havana Club, cola, and fresh fish. Then pack up all of your finds in a box made of sugar cane and take them home.*

José was the same age as my daughter, Angelica. At just thirteen years old, his whole world had turned upside down when both of his parents had been diagnosed with HIV/AIDS and forced to leave their family home to live in the sanatorium. He had been sent to boarding school. As I waited for him to return, I thought about my own children.

Angelica was fifteen years old when my husband, Clarence, was diagnosed with AIDS. We did not have the luxury of time to figure out how to tell her, my son, Jonah, and my stepdaughter, Kiwan, this terrible news. Clarence was seriously ill and already in the hospital when we gathered our three teenaged kids to inform them of his diagnosis. I remembered how difficult it was for me to find the right words—any words—to begin that conversation. I, at least, had the benefit of an internal process that had been going on for months during which Clarence had battled bouts of "flu" and unknown infections. I had begun to suspect, to fear, that we might be facing this moment—that he had not, as he'd always believed he would, escaped this bullet, the bullet of AIDS. But I had kept these thoughts to myself. For our kids there had been no preparation, and I wasn't really able to focus on supporting them or helping them through their fears. For several months, Clarence hovered on the edge, near death, and I simply moved forward each day to meet each new challenge until his condition stabilized and he began the long slow transition to becoming "a person living with AIDS." After he came home and we resumed some semblance of normal life, I assumed they were okay—I *needed* them to be okay.

What would my kids say now if I asked them the questions I planned to ask José? *How did you feel when you first heard of your father's diagnosis?* José had seen both his parents captured by this virus. I hadn't gotten tested myself until Clarence was out of the woods. I just couldn't bear the possibility at that time of having to deal with learning that I too had been infected. But my kids spent months wondering and worrying about me.

Did you tell anyone else that your parents had HIV/AIDS? My son shared the news with his college girlfriend, and she withdrew from him in a panic—terrified, despite information to the contrary, that this virus had somehow touched Jonah. My daughter, a sophomore in high school, hesitated to invite friends home where the unmistakable signs of illness would confront them—-a bed in the living room, hospital equipment scattered around the apartment, and Clarence, thin and weak, greeting them from his recliner. Kiwan, Clarence's daughter, felt angry and betrayed at one more way that her father had let her down. "It wasn't exactly the kind of thing you walked into the school cafeteria and said to your friends, 'Hey, guess what?'" she told me later.

Would these young people from very different cultures find common ground in their experience? José had been ten years old when his father, Orlando, volunteered for an international mission in Angola; he had been thirteen when Orlando returned, was diagnosed with HIV and sent to live in the AIDS sanatorium in Havana, and he was twenty-two when Orlando died. But José had endured more—his mother was also diagnosed with HIV and sent to live at Los Cocos, his family life was completely disrupted, he was sent to boarding school, and he became the keeper of a dark secret. How had all of this affected him? How did he view his own life?

José and I sat for a while talking in the small concrete yard behind the house. The sun was hot, and we had to raise our voices above the sounds of hammering and sawing from a construction project next door. José answered my questions directly in a rapid, guttural Spanish sprinkled with colloquial expressions and did not embellish much. He held the small tape recorder I used to record interviews close to his mouth. Caridad left us alone.

"I was ten years old when my father went to Angola," José began. "I missed him, but I felt proud of what he was doing. And I still had my mother." During the time that Orlando was away, Caridad and José continued living in their small family apartment on the top floor of a building in Centro Habana, a few blocks behind the *Capitolio*. "I went to school like always. I played sports. I helped my mom. The time went by fast."

José remembered going to see his father march in a big parade. Though Orlando had been a civilian mechanic and not a combatant, he was greeted, with the rest of his battalion, like a hero.

I was reminded of how different this was from how Clarence had felt when he returned from Vietnam. His mother told me that she had cooked a big dinner for him when he got back, and everyone dressed up like for a party to welcome him home, but Clarence was quiet and brooding. When she told him that she had received his Purple Heart from the Marine Corps, he demanded that she bring it to him. "And then he went in the back yard and tore it to pieces and just threw it away," she said. She was confused. She was proud of him. She didn't understand his anger.

José and I continued to talk, but he kept looking at his watch. He needed to pick his wife up from work and was getting concerned about the time. He emphasized, as his mother had, how important his friend's family had been in his life after his parents had gone to live in the sanatorium. "They were the only ones who knew what I was going through," he said. "I came here every weekend at first."

At this point in our conversation, some friends arrived and greeted José loudly, then clapped hands over their mouths as they realized they were interrupting an interview. José left to get his wife, and I rejoined Caridad and Carnota in the dark, cool living room. We would leave as soon as José got back to avoid the anxiety of making the trip back to Havana at night. If something happened to the car on the highway, it would be hard to get help in the dark.

The trunk of the car was loaded up with all of Carnota's loot—boxes of rum and cola, smelly fish wrapped in newspaper. Caridad kissed her son good-bye, holding him tight for a long embrace—they had come through so much together. All the way home, as dusk descended, I thought again about my own kids. Angelica was in college, Jonah was living in California with his Nicaraguan girlfriend, and Kiwan had a son of her own, Brandon, who looked a lot like the grandfather he would never know. When I got home we would sit and talk. José's story had reminded me of how important that was.

Caridad visits her son Jose as often as she can. When she was first admitted to the sanatorium, he had to be sent to a boarding school and the separation was wrenching for her.

CHAPTER FIFTEEN

WHY IS THIS NIGHT DIFFERENT?

The calendar I had brought from home to hang on the wall at Ruki's told me that it was the first night of Passover and I was unexpectedly seized with homesickness and longing. As a secular Jew, Passover is the only holiday I feel a real connection to—for both its ritual and its meaning. I had always found a way to attend or make a seder, but in Cuba? What were the chances?

My childhood Passovers were spent in the home of my great-grandparents, where my great uncles and aunts carried on the traditions they had learned. I have no memories of my great-grandfather, though I have seen photos of him. He married my parents in the small living room of that house, decorated with antique wooden furniture and treasures from the "old country"—a small village on the border of Poland and Russia whose boundaries shifted with the blowing winds of political change. He was a small man who wore the cap of an Orthodox rabbi, and carried that title, though he never received formal education. He fathered eleven children, some in that village who were brought here as children, and some in the new land of New England where the family settled. There is one picture in our family album of my great-grandfather holding me, a toddler, on his lap. He stares directly at the camera, a serious expression on his face. I am looking off to one side.

During those Passover seders, the whole large family gathered at a long table, cobbled together from every table in the house, that stretched from the musty sun porch, through the formal dining room and into the living room—furniture pushed aside to make room for four generations of Schwolskys. A separate table for the cousins—the kids—was set up at the end.

The seder itself seemed interminable and we squirmed and wriggled through it all—chanted in Hebrew by my great-grandfather, my great uncles, and my grandfather, the only generation that still observed the original rituals and could read the language. But I was caught, even then, by the idea of a holiday celebrating an escape from slavery to freedom. As that generation of the family grew old and died, my father took over the Passover celebration and we graduated from the leather-bound tomes of my great-grandfather to the Maxwell House Passover Haggadah, free in every supermarket that sold matzoh and gefilte fish for the traditional meal. My father, not one for extended ritual, moved quickly through the story so that we could get to the delicious food.

I couldn't imagine finding a seder in Havana, where the Jewish population had shrunk over the years to around 1,500, but what did I have to lose? I asked a co-worker, one of the psychologists at the sanatorium, who seemed to have wide knowledge of off-the-beaten-path events in the city.

"*Si, si, seguro que si,*" she told me. "There is a synagogue right near your apartment in Vedado, the Patronato. Just pass by there on your way home tonight. I think you will find what you are looking for, how do you call it, a seder."

I followed her instructions, which led me to the intersection of Calle I and 13th. The street was dark, the only light from a solitary streetlamp on the corner. I couldn't see the buildings well, let alone the numbers, and nothing looked like a synagogue.

An elderly man was sweeping the sidewalk in front of a building in the middle of the block.

"*Perdoname*, excuse me," I said as I approached. "I am looking for the Patronato, for a special *comida* they may be having tonight."

"*Ah si, seguro, el seder,*" he responded with a big smile. "*Tienes que entrar a esta puerta,*" pointing me to a door to what looked like it must be a basement, down a small flight of stairs.

"*Gracias, pero , , ,* am I too late? I don't have a reservation."

He laughed. "*Estas bienvenida siempre a cualquier hora,*" he said. You are always welcome at whatever hour.

I made my way down the stairs and pushed open the heavy wooden door to a room lit with candles. Long tables, covered with white tablecloths, formed a square in the middle of the room. The tables were full and the seder was underway. I turned to leave, embarrassed to have "crashed" this celebration, but a young man came to my side, welcomed me and, after learning that I was a North American living in Cuba, guided me to a spot at what looked to be the head table. Why is this night different from all other nights? I had found my seder in Havana.

Around the tables, which I now could see were set with all the trappings of a Passover seder—plates with matzoh, the flat unleavened bread that symbolizes the hasty flight of the Jews from Egypt; hardboiled eggs; a seder plate with all the symbols of the holiday. I picked up the printed and stapled Haggadah on my plate. It was in three languages—Hebrew, Spanish, and English—and it was then that I noticed the large group of *extranjeros* or foreigners seated around the table. Later I learned that they were from Minnesota, on a Jewish-heritage tour of Cuba.

Young men and women wearing yarmulkas, the saucer-shaped traditional head covering worn at synagogue and for religious celebrations, took their turns at a podium, reading out portions of the seder service in Spanish and Hebrew.

And then it was time for the meal—and what a meal it was. Gefilte fish and horseradish, followed by steaming bowls of chicken broth with matzoh balls floating within, roast chicken, fresh vegetables I hadn't seen in two months, and for dessert, bowls of delicious Cuban ice cream.

"But where did all this come from?" I whispered to my neighbor, a middle-aged woman who looked like she could have been the sister of my Aunt Margie.

"Canada," she replied, *"una synagoga en Canada nos mando todos los años."* A synagogue in Canada sent this feast—but how?—every year so that this small Jewish congregation could celebrate the seder. I was astounded and deeply moved.

Later my curiosity would lead me to visit other Jewish historical sites and explore more about the Jewish experience in Cuba. I would learn about the first Jews who came with Columbus, the Sephardic Jews who came in the 16th century to escape the persecution of the Spanish Inquisition, the Ashkenazik Jews who emigrated from Eastern Europe to escape the pogroms of the Czar, and finally, the tragic story of the SS St. Louis, a ship loaded with 937 passengers trying to escape Nazi Germany in 1939. Cuba was prepared to take them in, but the US discouraged this, perhaps fearing a precedent they would have to follow. The ship anchored in Havana harbor for a week while the issue was debated. In the end, entry to Cuba was refused and the ship was forced to return to Europe where the fate of the passengers was surely a tragic one.

Before the Revolution, Havana's Jewish community was reported to be 15,000 in number and supported five synagogues, several schools, and a college. Cuban Jews were, for the most part, successful in the garment business and led a cosmopolitan life. Many had brought their socialist ideals from Europe and were prominent in the founding of both the labor and the Cuban communist movements.

But with the Revolution, Cuba's Jews became part of the massive exile of the bourgeois class from the island and only a couple of thousand remained. They enjoyed freedom to practice their religion, when many others were barred from attending church or wearing Christian symbols. They even kept their religious schools open and the Cuban government provided buses.

At the time of my seder, in 1996, the Jewish community was experiencing a new growth, fueled mainly by young Cubans converting to Judaism—finding less restrictions in this new faith. Indeed, many of the young people at the seder were converts.

But that night, the night of the Passover seder, I wasn't thinking of history or politics. I was only happy to have found my tribe in Havana and a ritual that celebrated a struggle for freedom and a commitment to welcome the stranger that, for me, had always been what I treasured in my religious tradition.

"Let all who are hungry, come and eat," the seder commands. "And let every generation tell the story."

After the meal was over, lively conversations started up around the room. I was careful to introduce myself as "a judia from Nueva York," having learned from my previous mistake in which I had described myself as "jodia"—or all screwed up. The door to this Cuban Jewish community had been opened to me, a stranger, and I left that night, walking home through the darkened streets, savoring this surprising experience, the sweetness of the coconut macaroon cookies we had for dessert lingering in my mouth.

*Decorative gates mark the Patronato, the synagogue in Havana that
is the center of Jewish life on the island.*

CHAPTER SIXTEEN

NO WORD FOR QUILT

On an unusually hot afternoon in May, several weeks after I shared the photos of Clarence's quilt, a small group finally met to begin working on the first Cuban panel. There were six or seven of us crammed into the one tiny room of Jaime's house, at the very end of the path that leads from the clinic to the edge of Marañón. Jaime was not with us—he had, in fact, been studying in Colombia for over a year—and the house had seen a variety of inhabitants in that time, but remained in the eyes of everyone in the sanatorium "Jaime's house." This was like so many things in Cuba—constantly changing, yet always somehow the same.

But it became immediately clear that there would be some challenges in translating this uniquely American project into Cuban cultural reality. There was no tradition of quilting on this tropical island—not even a word in Cuban Spanish for "quilt." We tried *colcha*, which means "blanket," but it didn't convey the constructed patchwork of a quilt. The Mexican AIDS Quilt project used the word *manteles,* or shawls, which were part of Mexican burial rites, but this was not a familiar word for Cubans. Finally we settled for *paneles*, or panels, to describe in plain language the AIDS memorial we would create.

The idea was simple and powerful. A swath of black fabric was spread before us on the floor. "The size of the panel is the same size as a coffin," I explained, as we carefully cut it to the requisite six-foot-by-three-foot length. "The first panels were created in a living room like this one in San Francisco. Can you imagine there are now over ten thousand panels stored in a warehouse?"

Caridad had an idea for the design, which the group quickly approved. The island of Cuba would be outlined, with a royal palm tree rising up from the center. The leaves of the palm tree would bear the names of the six members of the Grupo de Prevención who had died since the group was founded in 1991—and they would look for a quotation or poem to go alongside the palm. Diego, who had been a tailor by profession before he moved into the sanatorium, had agreed to do most of the sewing.

"What do *you* think, Elena?" Alejandro asked.

"It's a beautiful idea," I replied. "My daughter will be here in a couple of weeks with some new fabric and threads. In the meantime, we can work on the design. Are we ready to get started?"

But doubts had begun to surface. Should we get permission to make the panel? From whom? "They probably won't ever let us display it anyway, so why bother making it?" one person suggested. And another chimed in, "We'd better be sure we get approval or it can really cause problems for the group." The AIDS Prevention Group were volunteers—some living in the sanatorium and others in their communities—who were doing their work with the support and approval of the Ministry of Health. But in Cuba, as I had been learning, many activities of daily life were governed by a complex set of spoken and unspoken rules and agreements.

We seemed to be stalled before we even really began, and I was at a loss to know what to do. I wanted to urge them on—let's just do it and deal with all that later—but I was hesitant to voice my opinion. I was sure that there was something I was missing, not understanding.

Who was I to push this Cuban group beyond boundaries that I didn't even really comprehend?

We stopped the discussion for icy glasses of thick fresh papaya juice brought by a neighbor and then wandered outside looking for relief from the stifling heat. A faint breeze stirred the mangoes, still green and holding fast to their branches high overhead. The black, coffin-sized cloth waited inside for the design of our memories to take shape.

It was a little more than two years after Clarence's death, in the summer of 1992, that I had gathered a group of friends in my kitchen to begin designing the AIDS Quilt panels we would make for him. I knew a little about the history of the quilt—how in 1985, a man named Cleve Jones and a small group of his friends had written the names of their loved ones who had died of AIDS on coffin-sized plac-ards and carried them into the streets during a candlelight march. At the end of the march, they taped the placards to the wall of the Federal Building. The wall of names looked like a patchwork quilt. A year later they made the first fabric panels. The idea caught on and the quilt had grown by thousands each year and traveled to displays all across the country.

I had never been to a display of the quilt, but had participated in quilting bees with families from the clinic as they sewed panels for their loved ones. Now it was my turn. The next big national display of the AIDS Quilt was scheduled for October of that year, and I wanted Clarence's panel to be there.

We were surrounded by piles of Clarence's T-shirts on the table, on chairs, on the floor. I had hung on to them long after I gave away everything else because they represented all the different aspects of his life to me—and now I was so glad that I had. We had sorted through the shirts that very afternoon, maybe a hundred of them, and chosen his beloved Brooklyn Dodgers, the WBGO JazzFest, End Apartheid in bold red on a yellow background, Vietnam Veterans Against the War, Narcotics Anonymous . . . I liked the idea that the most vital parts of Clarence's life would be represented by shirts that he had worn every day.

My friend Susan, an amateur quilter, helped me select an African fabric for the background and we painstakingly cut and stitched the logo from each shirt into a colorful fabric square. Then we sewed them all together to make the quilt panel, bordered by the brilliant red and orange African pattern. Clarence's mother sat in the recliner in the corner, the same one he had occupied so often during the last months of his life, making a panel for her son. She bent her cottony white head over the blue cloth, stitching black felt letters that spelled out the names of all of his sisters, nieces and nephews—seventeen in all. His four sisters created their own panel on a black background with painted symbols—"We miss the sun in your face, the stars in your eyes and the rainbow of things you do to keep us happy."

And our goddaughter Shannon, who was eight at the time, painted a colorful tree with deep roots on her panel and wrote a poem in her childish scrawl—the last line echoing my own longing: *"Boy, do I wish he was still living."*

When we were finished, we wrapped each of the four panels we had created in tissue paper, packed them carefully together, and sent them off to San Francisco. By then, the panels had become alive for me, yet another part of Clarence that I had to say good-bye to . . . but I knew that I would see them again in a few months at the national AIDS Quilt display.

On a cloudy October day, I wandered the Washington Mall in a daze, Clarence's "block" number 02459 scribbled on a piece of paper clutched tightly in my hand. The quilt panels were sewn together in groups of eight, forming twelve-by-twelve-foot blocks with white plastic walkways between them. A box of tissues was carefully placed at a corner of each block, and white-clad volunteers moved around the quilt, helping visitors find their panels and offering quiet support. The sound of the names being read over the loudspeaker system drifted over my head as I walked, barely glancing at the panels on either side of me which stretched in seemingly endless rows from one end of the Mall to the other.

When I finally found Clarence's block, I dropped to my knees on the damp grass, patting the quilt panel, straightening it, laughing, crying. Clarence's four panels shared a block with four others. This seemed strange to me at first. Who were these people sharing Clarence's memorial? In one corner, a blue fabric rectangle bore the name "*Nicholas Schaffner*" appliquéd in large cursive letters. Who was he and who had made his panel? The other three bright red panels represented babies and children from the New York City Foster Grandparents program. Their names and ages, ranging from four months to eight years, were scattered across the fabric with stars and angels and rainbows—and, in one corner, the golden arches of McDonalds with a puffy cloth hamburger and felt French fries peeking out of a red cloth box. It seemed fitting somehow that Clarence would be joined to all of these kids. He came from a large family, eleven brothers and sisters in all, and was often in the midst of an assortment of nieces and nephews—"knuckleheads" as he called them, all vying for his attention.

I stayed with Clarence's panels a long time that day. All around me, a thousand different scenes of loss and loving memory were being acted out. A silver-haired woman stood by a neighboring panel and proudly introduced her son to everyone who passed by.

"This is my son, Bobby. He was an artist. He loved color, that's why I tried to put a lot of color into his panel."

Small clusters of people gathered at every square. A tall, gaunt man stood silent and alone, with a single red rose in his hand. After a very long time, he laid it down on the panel in front of him and moved on down the row.

And through that whole long day the reading of the names went on and on, like a river of memories flowing through our hearts.

Back in Jaime's living room, the group had decided to move forward. We started by unfolding the black cloth we would use as our background. The air was still and heavy, and we had to keep wiping away droplets of sweat to keep them from falling on the fabric that was spread at our feet. People were coming and going all afternoon—popping their heads in for a moment to see how we were doing, running off to look for a favorite scrap of cloth to add to the panel or a vaguely remembered line of poetry to contribute. Sergio disappeared for an hour, returning at last with a gaudy length of golden lace—the long-treasured fringe from his grandmother's bedspread—that he added to the growing jumble of material on the floor. A large sheet of paper had to be found, and pencils, and someone who could draw a reasonable likeness of *la isla*.

Several people had a go at the outline of the island before we were satisfied and ready to trace it onto the teal-colored cloth we had selected for that purpose. My daughter Angelica's visit, when she would bring the fabric I had requested, was still a few weeks away, so we had to make do with what we had. Not an inch of fabric could be wasted—there would be no easy way to replace it at a time when everything in Cuba was patched and recycled a dozen times before being discarded. The design had to be traced with a strong, sure hand—the first cut into the fabric committing us somehow to this project that had begun with such halting steps.

"I still think they'll never let us show this in public." Alejandro had joined us after work and was perched on the arm of a chair, sharing his strong opinion. Our blue-green island had, by that time, been freed from its cloth boundary and placed carefully in the center of a black rectangular sea. We were gathered around admiring our work, but Alejandro' words fell on us like a heavy blanket in the heat of the afternoon. The intense energy and activity of drawing and cutting ceased abruptly. A ripple of doubt spread around the room.

Caridad weighed in from the kitchen where she was washing up the remains of our coffee break. "We should have waited for *permiso* before we started; I thought so from the beginning."

"What do you think, Elenita?" Hermes asked. "Maybe we should wait until we get the authorization." I wanted to scream. We seemed to have finally overcome the self-censure and uncertainty that Cubans navigated daily to actually begin the project, and this spreading wave of doubt threatened to stop us. What harm could it do, I wanted to plead, a rectangle of cloth with a design on it, a way to remember?

Then my own doubts overtook me again. Who was I to urge them on? The *extranjera* who would be leaving in a month, returning to a different set of rules? The AIDS Quilt could be viewed as yet another *American* project being imposed on Cuba. Maybe they *would* get in trouble for making the panel—at worst, privileges could be denied, or all of the effort could be for nothing, and the panel could sit folded at the bottom of a box, never shared, another example of initiative thwarted by bureaucracy and fear.

"Maybe we won't get permission to display it," I began, "but does it really matter? We're doing this to remember Orlando and Niurka and Alexei and the others. We're creating the panel together to heal ourselves. Why not keep going and see what happens? We've made such a good start."

Alejandro shrugged, giving tacit approval to my plea, and the group slowly resumed work. Diego began to draw the majestic royal palm that was to grow out of the center of our green island. Its leaves would bear the names of the six members of the Grupo de Prevención who would be memorialized by this panel—Alcides, Malina, Alexei, Orlando, Raul, and Niurka. Sergio's golden fringe framed the poems we had selected to take their place on either side of the palm. Like the first quilt panel created in San Francisco more than a decade ago, we had made a small beginning in this Cuban living room in Los Cocos.

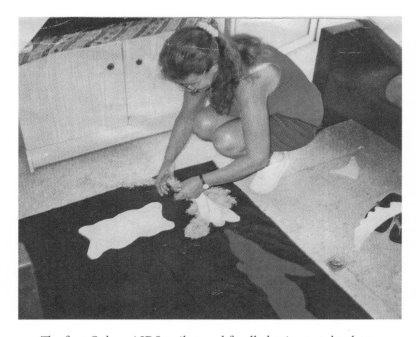

The first Cuban AIDS quilt panel finally begins to take shape.

CHAPTER SEVENTEEN

UNA YUMA IN HAVANA

C*hile? Argentina?* These words were shouted out by two teenage boys walking behind me as I made my way home from the sanatorium one afternoon. *How could they tell from behind?* I wondered. I was wearing old faded jeans and sneakers, a nondescript blouse, and carrying my well-worn backpack. And yet these two boys knew right away that I was foreign, not Cuban. They continued their search for a country that would produce a fair-skinned, European-looking woman. *Italia? Rusa? Americana*, I said as they pulled up to walk beside me. *Gringa*, I added with a smile. And then we were off. *Do you live in Miami? No, New Jersey. New Jersey? Then you must know my tía, Carmen. . . .*

There were tourists in Cuba in increasing numbers by 1996—mostly from Spain and Italy. Tour groups also regularly arrived from Canada, Mexico, and other parts of Latin America. I even ran into a couple of camera-laden groups from Japan in Old Havana one day. New luxury hotels were opening and older budget models being refurbished in Havana and along the seacoast. But Americans were still forbidden by the US government to travel to Cuba as tourists, so it was a novelty to encounter an American in Havana—especially one who was not part of one of the political tours or illicitly visiting a beach resort at Varadero. Although I much preferred a more anonymous existence and made a big effort to fit in and not draw attention to myself, I was trying to stay open to these street encounters and the curiosity I attracted. They often provided an opportunity to learn things I would not glean from my more formal work relationships.

I frequently used the word "gringa" to refer to my status as a foreigner, and one from the US. It was a word I had heard used in travel to Mexico and Nicaragua, but, as my Cuban friends explained, it was not a word that was used in Cuba. *Yuma* was the Cuban vernacular and it could refer to the place or the person. So I was, in fact, a *Yuma* in Havana, who came from and would return to the *Yuma*. But why *Yuma?* As legend has it, the word comes from an American western movie, 3:10 to Yuma, which became a hit in Havana in 1957. Cuban teenagers began using "Yuma" for the United States shortly after Fidel Castro took power in 1959, not knowing that it referred to a small town in Arizona. The term became widespread in 1980 when Cubans seeking asylum crashed a minibus through the Peruvian Embassy gates in Havana, and thousands more joined them, asking to go to "La Yuma."

But being from the *Yuma* had no effect on the generosity with which I was treated by everyday Cubans I met. One day I was waiting in a typical line for the *guagua*, the bus that would take me to an event at a hospital in central Havana. The Prevention Group had been invited to meet with the administration because this was the hospital that cared for many of the patients who had left the sanatorium, and there had been some problems with fear and prejudice on the part of the staff. We would conduct a session on living with HIV/AIDS, and they had asked me to present my slide show on pediatric AIDS.

The bus route was unfamiliar to me, and I was anxious about getting there on time. I managed the required *Quien es el último?* (Who is last on line?) and *Detrás de quien?* (Behind whom?) to find and mark my place in the loosely assembled group waiting for the bus.

Perhaps my accent gave me away, or my apparent lack of familiarity with this ritual. In any case, an older gentleman standing near me at the bus stop asked if he could be of help. *Americana?* he asked, figuring me out right away. *De donde? Turista?* I briefly described my work and what I was doing in Cuba, and we launched into a deep conversation about health care in Cuba, life in the US, and the politics of the embargo, which helped pass the twenty minutes or so before the bus arrived.

Like most buses in Havana in those days, it was jammed. I lost sight of my new friend for a moment while I engaged in the decidedly Cuban practice of passing my bus fare up from hand to hand to the conductor at the front. "Does this bus go to Hospital Miguel Enríquez and can you please tell me what stop to get off at?" I asked the person next to me.

My new friend responded from somewhere behind me in this sea of sweaty bodies. "I am going there myself. I will take you." I relaxed a bit—another Cuban experience successfully navigated. I waited for his signal to get off the bus.

We disembarked on a leafy street in front of the imposing hospital building. "*Quiere un cafécito?*" Before I could answer, my friend put a steaming little cup of rich dark espresso coffee into my hands, purchased from a vendor in front of the hospital. "I know the vice-director of this hospital," he told me. "I had surgery here. Why don't I take you in and introduce you?" The next thing I knew, I was being shepherded into a large office and greeted by the director of the hospital. Coffee was served (again—there was always coffee!), and this busy doctor took more than half an hour out of his day to entertain an unannounced American visitor. My friend excused himself at the beginning of our conversation, but not before handing me a piece of paper on which he had written his name and address in Havana and his daughter's name and address in Santiago, on the other side of the island. "She is a *médico de la familia*, a family doctor," he told me, "and if you get to Santiago you can stay with her. Just call her up."

This easy familiarity and extension of hospitality was repeated wherever I traveled in Cuba. First, curiosity, followed by questions, then in many cases, an invitation to visit the family, come to dinner, take a letter back to my uncle in Union City. From Ruki, my landlady's morning march through my bedroom to look out my windows onto the street, to my sleepovers at my friend María Luisa's where I shared their one bedroom with María Luisa and her husband, mother, and daughter, to my neighbor's shouted invitation to the family doctor passing by that one of the neighbors (whom she named at full volume) didn't look well and he should stop by to see her—all of my often unconscious norms about privacy were challenged on a daily basis. I wondered how much of this behavior had deep roots in Cuban culture and how much had been influenced by the collective values of a socialist society. In my travels in other parts of the world—Spain, Nicaragua, Puerto Rico, Jamaica—I had often been met with a more suspicious regard than I found here in Cuba.

Sometimes this open sharing could be uncomfortable, as it was one Saturday when I decided to act more like a tourist and take a ferry trip to Regla, a neighborhood across the bay where Santeria culture flourished. I planned to walk the streets a bit and visit a small museum. I got up very early, packed a small snack to take with me— as it was impossible to predict if food would be available—and set out for the ferry. As the small boat pulled away from the dock in Havana, I heard the sounds of muffled crying from behind me. I was alone on the bow of the ship with a young woman who was huddled on a bench and sobbing inconsolably. Between sobs, she glanced up at me. "*Americana*? *Mi prima*, my cousin, lives in New York. Do you know New York"? I told her a little bit about where I was from and what I was doing in Cuba, and she began, slowly at first, and then without pause, to tell me her story.

She talked nonstop, and by the time we docked, I had learned that this woman was a doctor. (In Cuba it sometimes seemed like everyone was a doctor!) She was returning home after having just worked a night shift at a hospital in Havana. She was very upset, she told me, because she had recently learned that her husband was having an affair. She was returning to his parents' apartment where they lived together with their eighteen-month-old daughter to pack up her things and move out. She was not sure where she would go. She had no family in Havana. Maybe she would stay with a friend from the hospital for a while until she figured things out. In addition to the affair, which maybe she could forgive, her husband had been physically abusive to her. She lifted a sleeve of the white lab coat she was still wearing and showed me a large bruise around her wrist. That she would never forgive.

The whole trip had taken about fifteen minutes, and I had learned intimate details of a stranger's personal crisis. As we prepared to disembark, she scrawled her name and the address of the hospital where she worked on a piece of paper. "Come and visit me anytime. I will show you around the hospital," she promised and then was off up the hill to pack up her life.

Of course, not all street encounters with strangers were productive or pleasant. Often I was followed by persistent black-market vendors who were hard to shake off. Or young men who were suspiciously anxious to make my acquaintance. During this period of material scarcity, having a friend who was an *extranjera* or foreigner could mean gifts of hard to obtain food or clothing for your family. In the early 1990s, at the beginning of the Special Period, it was illegal for Cubans to have dollars in their possession, yet the dollar was the only currency that could buy anything. So often when I visited the Dollar Stores, set up for tourists and diplomats, I would have to wade through a group of Cubans asking me to take their illicit dollars and buy them a particular item in the store.

Similarly, Cubans were not allowed in the tourist hotels or restaurants. Some critics at the time referred to this policy as a type of "tourist apartheid," and it always made me intensely uncomfortable, especially when I was staying in a hotel and it meant that I could not reciprocate the generosity of my Cuban friends by inviting them to visit or have dinner with me. At the same time, Cuban authorities seemed to look the other way when the young jineteras plied their trade with European businessmen or tourists.

I spent the first few months in Cuba trying desperately to blend in, but my friend Betts took a totally different approach. I first met Betts about halfway through my six-month stay. An improbable pair anywhere else but in Havana, we began to pal around on weekends and meet occasionally during the week to compare notes and vent. Betts was an American doing research for a PhD dissertation that took her into the frustratingly bureaucratic circles of economic planning and labor. In her spare time, to recover, she often biked out to visit organic gardening projects on the outskirts of Havana.

Betts stood out in a Cuban crowd. Her way of negotiating the Cuban scene was refreshing and interesting to me. Neither of us was cut from tourist cloth, and that was certainly obvious to curious Cuban observers. But while I aimed at attracting nothing more than a cursory glance or a raised eyebrow from passersby attempting to guess my origins and what I was doing in Cuba, Betts trumpeted her difference, tramping the streets in long flowered skirts, tank tops, and hiking boots. While I worked on perfecting my accent and colloquialisms to the point that people often assumed I was from somewhere in Latin America, Betts blundered into conversation in her unmistakably northern-accented tones. She refused to suffer the hundreds of daily absurdities of life in Cuba with a properly patient attitude, and she complained about Cubans all the time. Hanging out with her turned my culturally sensitive world upside down, but I liked it.

A few weeks after I met Betts, my daughter, Angelica, came down for a visit. I had been planning to spend the time with her in Havana, but Betts suggested we take a trip around the island.

"Really?" I asked. "That seems challenging."

"Just rent a car and go," Betts said, with her typical bravado. "I'll help you plan a route. Hell, I'll even go with you if you want me to."

Angelica and I spent a week in Havana, a whirlwind of visits to friends, nights strolling on the Malecón, a trip to one of the eastern beaches near Havana. She delivered the beautiful lengths of fabric she had brought to an excited group at the sanatorium, along with the two rubber penises I had requested. Then the three of us set off in a small VW sedan to see the island. We made a circle from Havana to Santa Clara, famous as the site of the last battle of the Cuban Revolution in 1958, to the beautiful colonial city of Trinidad, and then on to the famous beach resort of Varadero. Following Betts's lead, we didn't make reservations ahead of time but took our chances with small budget hotels.

In the province of Villa Clara, about an hour from Varadero, we stumbled upon an old hotel and spa from Cuba's Russian-influenced era. "Mud baths!" Betts exclaimed. "We have to do it." The next day we were guided around a circuit of crumbling installations—hot springs, mineral springs, and of course, the mud baths. Angelica made sure the photos taken that day of the three of us in bathing suits, slathered from head to toe in black gooey mud, never saw the light of day.

Soon after Angelica's visit, Betts moved out of the Cuban home where she had been renting a room and into a cottage on the outskirts of the city—a forty-five-minute bike ride each way. The first time we biked out there together, Betts neglected to tell me that she was a triathlon competitor back home in New Mexico. Lean and muscular, deeply tanned, with a long blond frizzy braid halfway down her back, skirt hitched up for maximum comfort, she wheeled aggressively through the bumpy Havana streets with me tagging slightly behind, red-faced and breathless from my effort to keep up. On these excursions, blending in was not an option.

Betts was a vegetarian in a country obsessed with meat. One day we visited the local farmers' market to gather ingredients for a vegetable stew. I moved timidly between the stalls with my Cuban pesos trying not to attract the attention of hustlers and black marketeers. Betts, on the other hand, boldly questioned the quality of the merchandise, haggled loudly over prices, and brushed off the hustlers with an impatient and slightly imperious wave of her hand. We emerged with armloads of eggplant, having taken the farmers' market by storm.

When I spent time with Betts, I got to whine and complain in English. This was an enormous relief after days spent speaking and hearing only Spanish, struggling to absorb and understand every cultural and linguistic nuance, and trying hard not to break any of the informal and formal rules of Cuban society.

We would sit on the patio of Betts's little bourgeois cottage after a selfishly indulgent and very un-Cuban meal, sipping *mojitos*, a delicious drink reputed to be Hemingway's favorite: rum, mineral water, sugar, lime juice, angostura, and fresh mint. And we'd trade complaints until the mosquitoes finally drove us inside.

"Sometimes I feel invisible here—I wish people would show more interest in my dreams, what hardships I've had in my life, what my life is like back home," I would tentatively begin. Betts would match and raised my complaint with a story that illustrated just how opinionated and stubborn Cubans can be. And so the evening wound pleasantly on.

It was during one such late-night session that Betts said something that would stay with me through all the ups and downs of the quilt project. The project had been stalled again for a couple of weeks while everyone tried to figure out whose permission we needed to proceed. I was frustrated with the passivity of the group. Why couldn't we just make the first panel like we had planned and then see what would happen? The panel was half finished, waiting for someone at a higher level to give it his or her blessing.

"I can't stand it," I lamented to Betts one evening on her patio. "It's such a simple thing, making a panel to remember people who have died of AIDS, and we can't do it without permission. I don't understand what's the big deal? It's making me crazy."

"Here's what I think about how things work in Cuba," she said, slapping at mosquitoes and taking another sip of her rum and Coke. "If someone doesn't say you have permission to do something, and better yet put it in writing, then you assume that you can't do it and that something reasonably terrible may befall you if you do. Whereas in the good old US of A, we assume we can do whatever we goddamn please unless someone tells us we can't. That's the difference between here and there."

Simple enough, and maybe not up to the standards of Betts's exactingly elitist doctoral committee, but that thought helped me both see what I was up against and figure out how to move forward. I would be direct and lay down a challenge to the group. "Look, I'm leaving in a few weeks. Let's finish this now and then you can figure out what to do with it after I'm gone. But at least you'll have it. Our first panel. Our beautiful memorial." But first I would make sure Alejandro was on my side.

Betts' free-spirited approach to life in Cuba was infectious.

CHAPTER EIGHTEEN
PROYECTO MEMORIAS

I never got a chance to try out my new strategy and I never had to convince Alejandro that we should move ahead with the quilt project. He came bouncing in with big news after one of our class sessions at Los Cocos. We had finally not only gotten permission to go on working on the quilt, but we had received a special invitation to display the first panel at the celebration of the tenth anniversary of the sanatorium, to be held on April 30th. Diego the tailor had completed work on the panel over the weekend, and everyone was excited to see the results. All of the group's anxieties melted away as we prepared for the event—gently ironing the last wrinkles from the panel, deciding who would carry it to the front of the auditorium, writing a little speech of dedication.

The group decided that María Antonia, the psychologist, would begin by speaking about the history and activities of the Grupo de Prevención. Then several members would walk the panel down through the auditorium to the front where it would be presented, and we would ask for a moment of silence to remember those who had died.

"Sometimes at these events we invite people to speak the name of someone they want to remember out loud," I told the group, unsure if this would be appropriate at a formal Cuban celebration. "I love the idea," María Antonia responded enthusiastically, and the group continued preparations—selecting the music to be played and choosing those who would have the honor of carrying the panel.

The anniversary celebration was held several days later in the auditorium of the sanatorium and attended by most of the residents and staff, as well as some visiting dignitaries from the Ministry of Health. These kinds of events in Cuba tended to be very stiff and formal, and this was no exception. Noisy fans did little to move the stifling air in the auditorium as the usual speeches and awards for exemplary work were presented, and then it was our group's turn. María Antonia began to speak about the history of the Prevention Group over a soundtrack of Cuban piano music that swelled to a crescendo as we held the panel high and carried it proudly down the aisle. Caridad was at one end, Hermes at the other, while several of us held it taut in the center. A moment of silence was observed followed by the "naming" of those who were being remembered. After a slow and hesitant start, names were called out from all corners of the auditorium, by patients, doctors, nurses, cafeteria workers. Caridad read our dedication. "With tears in our eyes, with a mixture of sadness and happiness, we present this first panel. We have decided to give the name *Memorias* to our project here in Cuba because it makes us remember our partners, friends, brothers, and all of the loved ones who have died with AIDS."

The celebration ended with tears and hugs around the room—a poignant reminder that AIDS in Cuba was so much more than the controversy about quarantine and mass screening, that it was also a story of human suffering, loss, and courage, as it was all over the world. The group had taken a risk in beginning *Proyecto Memorias*, a risk that it would be misunderstood and perhaps even curtailed, but this Cuban audience had responded from the heart and embraced our quilt of remembrance.

Several weeks later, it was finally time for me to return home to

New Jersey. I spent my remaining days going through my fieldwork notes and taped interviews, tying up loose ends, and giving away the few belongings I had acquired during my stay. The Flying Pigeon bicycle went to Ruki's son Miguel.

I would be leaving a few days after May Day and really wanted to attend the celebration. May Day was celebrated as International Workers' Day in many places around the world. Cuba usually mounted a grand parade in Havana with marching bands, military pomp and circumstance, and contingents of children and workers from schools and workplaces all across the island. Due to the economic crisis, the parade had not been held for the last two years, but this year a big event was planned. There were smaller parades in local communities for a week leading up to the event, and meetings of the unions and neighborhood councils to mobilize people.

At first I had trouble finding someone who wanted to go with me—Ruki and her kids politely declined, saying that they would watch it on TV. Other friends laughed a little at my naïveté. They had long ago become cynical about such displays of revolutionary fervor. Finally I was invited to go with Carestina, a friend who was a nurse at the Tropical Medicine Institute.

It was a beautiful day, sunny, not too hot, and there were tens of thousands in the streets—work groups, school groups, neighborhood groups, bands, hundreds on bikes—a gigantic parade. We found a small group from the sanatorium huddled under the shade of a tree waiting for the march to begin. Carestina and I were excited, but it was clear some were there more for show. Alex the psychologist looked around for the sanatorium *jefes* so he could be sure they knew he was there (reminding me of some less-than-enthusiastic health-care-union constituents back home in New York during the Labor Day Parade). Soon we joined the march, walking down the grand boulevard lined with government buildings that led to Revolution Square. Groups of *Pioneros*, Cuba's patriotic scout troops, lined the route in their uniforms. I remembered their red and blue scarves from the Venceremos Brigade. Teachers were represented, and athletes, factory workers, doctors and nurses in their white lab coats, and throngs of schoolchildren.

As we approached the reviewing stand where Fidel was seated, we were suddenly off and running—being moved quickly past the site by Cuban soldiers. I wondered why. Security? Crowd control? I thought I caught a blurred glimpse of "*nuestro comandante y jefe*" Fidel Castro, and later stood for hours in the hot sun with hundreds of thousands of Cubans to listen to one of his very long speeches. I could imagine Ruki's son Miguel at home watching on TV and rolling his eyes at this somewhat bombastic event. But despite all I knew about the contradictions in Cuba's socialist experiment and the difficulties of daily life I had witnessed and experienced, I was deeply moved by this May Day celebration. There was still a collective spirit here—a commitment to make life better for everyone that seemed authentic and meaningful—and a fierce determination to remain independent and free from US domination.

Saying good-bye meant an endless round of visits and dinners where I was loaded up with letters to deliver to family members in the States. There was no direct mail service between the US and Cuba, and the only way to be sure a letter would arrive was to send it with a willing traveler. I was overwhelmed by the warmth and hospitality of my Cuban friends, but I quickly learned that I had started my leave-taking too soon. "When are you leaving, Elena?" Alejandro's mother asked, looking up from a letter she was finishing as we sat around after dinner one night.

"In a couple of days," I replied, not quite believing it myself.

"Well, you have to come and see us the day before your flight to say good-bye," she said, and I knew I would have to make yet another round of visits as I struggled to separate myself from my Cuban friends.

When I headed for the airport a few days later, in the 1940s-era Ford taxi that Ruki arranged, my luggage was several duffel bags lighter than when I'd arrived and my heart was heavy with nostalgia and regret. My life in the US had been filled with graduate school and work with little room for anything else for the past few years. I would miss the lively social whirl and deep connections of my life in Cuba.

Less than an hour later, I found myself in the airport in the Bahamas preparing for the usual US customs routine, which could be pretty nerve-wracking. I had traveled to Cuba "illegally" several times in the previous five years and waited nervously for the customs official's question: "Did you enjoy your trip to the Bahamas? Did you visit anywhere outside the Bahamas on this trip?" This time around, I was "legal," with a license for research in Cuba, but the nerves were still there. *Would travel to Cuba ever be normal?* I wondered as I opened my bag for inspection.

Another short flight and I was "home"—back in the US, waiting for my flight to New York in the Miami airport. The glitz and busy commerce that surrounded me were overwhelming, and I found myself a quiet corner to curl up in for a while. Before the next leg of the journey, I bought a Cuban sandwich from a booth in the airport—crusty bread layered with richly-spiced pork, cheese, and pickles—a sandwich impossible to find in Havana in those days, but readily available in the Miami airport.

I had always experienced a certain amount of culture shock when I returned from even short trips to Cuba, but this time I felt dislocated for weeks. I wandered into the Pathmark supermarket in Montclair and right back out again, overwhelmed by the aisles and aisles of breakfast cereals, breads, packaged meats, and heaping piles of fruits and vegetables. I tried to answer questions about Cuba from my coworkers and friends but found myself at a loss for ways to explain the nuances of the life I observed and lived there. My life in New Jersey felt so compartmentalized and isolated to me. I quickly returned to my work, school, and home routine. But it felt empty.

It was not long before this familiar routine was disrupted. The hospital where I had worked for almost ten years went bankrupt and soon closed. And my friends Tami and Karen, from whom I had been renting several rooms in the attic of their large home, decided to sell the house and move to Brooklyn. Just a few short months after my homecoming from Cuba, I found myself looking for a new home and a new job.

I landed temporarily in the spare room of a friend after the house was sold, and was surviving on unemployment benefits with just a semester left to complete in my master's program. I spent my days writing cover letters and finishing my schoolwork, including the journal and report that I had to turn in to get credit for my fieldwork.

Each night, at a card table desk in my little room, I began the work of transcribing the tapes of my interviews in Cuba. The sound of Caridad's soft voice or Alejandro's confident and rapid cadence transported me back to Los Cocos and carried me through the most difficult times. I received an occasional letter sent with someone coming back from a trip to Cuba and managed to get in touch by phone several times over the summer. In this way, I learned that word of our quilt project was spreading, and panels were arriving sent by mothers, lovers, and friends from all over the island. Caridad had finished her panel for Orlando with the purple orchid painted in the center. Diego, the tailor who helped us with the first panel, had made one for Alberto, his partner of many years. *Proyecto Memorias* was slowly growing.

Halfway through the summer, I learned that there was to be a national display of the AIDS Memorial Quilt in Washington, DC, in October, and that it might well be the last time the quilt was ever displayed in its entirety—it had simply gotten too big. One of the newsletters that I received about the October quilt display mentioned that there would be quilt panels from all over the world—and for the first time I learned of the existence of the International Names Project. Could Proyecto Memorias somehow be a part of this? What would it take to get the Cuban panels here? I was thrilled by the possibilities of this idea and began to figure out how to make it happen. Of course, the path was bumpy and full of potholes caused by the political situation between the US and Cuba. Who would bring the quilt panels and participate in the event? The group in Cuba selected Alejandro and Caridad to represent them. Hermes was eager to come, but because of his father's status he would never be able to obtain permission from the Cuban government. Now I had to find an organization in the US that would issue an invitation. The US + Cuba Medical Project, which provided humanitarian medical aid, agreed, and the Names Project wrote a letter of support. With this in hand, we could apply for visas for the trip. But it had to be completely paid for by the sponsoring organization—travel, lodging and all expenses—so we began a campaign to raise the $4000 to $5000 needed to fund the trip.

On a chilly day in October, I stood in the waiting area of Reagan International Airport in Washington, DC, anxiously awaiting the arrival of Alejandro and Caridad. Finally I spotted them, looking dazed and confused in the midst of the fast-moving crowds, grabbed their borrowed suitcases, and scooted them toward the exit. As we drove to the apartment we would be sharing for the week, they chattered like kids on a school field trip, amazed by the majestic boulevards of the capital, by the hectic pace of the traffic, by the signs of affluence everywhere. Alejandro had traveled outside of Cuba once—to Moscow—but this was Caridad's first trip ever off the island.

Alejandro and Caridad were immediately drawn into a whirl of activity with the International Quilt. As their host, I was honored to be included in some of the events, but they went alone to special workshop sessions for HIV+ people and were trained as volunteers to participate in the opening ceremony. We met panel-makers from projects in Mexico, Israel, Belgium, and South Africa. Souvenir pins and postcards were exchanged and deep bonds forged in just a few days. We made a display on foam board with a Cuban flag and photos of the Cuban quilt panels for an exposition of the International Quilt. I wandered down the aisle one day past the booths of the Irish Names Quilt, *Projecto des Noms* from Spain, and *Fundacíon Marozo* from Venezuela. And there sat Caridad, behind a table displaying the few AIDS education materials they were able to bring, with her serious face, next to a display of Proyecto Memorias. I was filled with pride at what we had achieved.

I took Alejandro and Caridad to visit Clarence's panels, the ones they had seen in photos at the sanatorium that had planted the seed that would grow into Proyecto Memorias. It was as if they were meeting Clarence in person and deepening their understanding of my experience. We fumbled in our fanny packs for the tissues we carried as quilt volunteers as the tears flowed freely.

The ten-day trip went by in a blur, and too soon it was time for Alejandro and Caridad to return to Cuba. We spent the night before their flight trying to stuff all of the new possessions they had acquired into newly purchased duffel bags—souvenirs of the quilt, toiletries, and clothing they had bought to bring back to family, as well as donated medications for AIDS patients in Cuba. And then it was time to say good-bye once more.

"When will we see each other again, Elenita?" Caridad asked in her quiet voice.

I was wondering the same thing. "Soon," I murmured. "Soon, I hope." But it would be almost a year before I returned to Cuba

We proudly hold aloft the first panel of Proyecto Memorias at the
event marking the 10ᵗʰ Anniversary of the Sanatorium.

CHAPTER NINETEEN

UNFOLDING

By the time we arrived at the plaza in front of the *Capitolio*, the first early morning travelers were already lining up at the bus stop across the street. A cafeteria on the corner opened its wooden shutters, and the smell of coffee drifted into the air, mixing with diesel fumes from the occasional trucks lumbering by. Streaks of pink were visible in the gray sky over Havana as the sun rose over the sea. The large open plaza was empty, except for an old woman who had begun to sweep the broken concrete and a solitary soldier leaning on his bike in the corner. Someone unfurled a banner: "*Proyecto Memorias: Grupo de Prevención SIDA, Habana.*" It was Sunday, the tenth of August, 1997, and the first public display of the AIDS Memorial Quilt in Cuba was about to begin.

Caridad, Hermes, and I huddled together on the steps leading up to the old Capitol, a building ironically modeled after its US counterpart, drinking steaming cups of café con leche and going over the schedule for the day. Just before nine, the bus from Los Cocos pulled up, and Alejandro jumped out, bullhorn in hand, already barking orders at the volunteers who were beginning to assemble. A few curious passersby stopped to watch as we unloaded the large fabric bundles from the bus and began to place them carefully around the square.

Alejandro's mother, sisters, nieces, and nephews arrived in what looked like a clown car—a car with a small metal covered wagon added on where the trunk would be—and piled out one by one, making us all laugh with the wonder of how they had managed to pack themselves in. They were there to help, as were María Luisa and Lucía, who set up a sewing machine on the steps to begin work on a panel for a *compañero* from the theater troupe.

Caridad handed me her coffee cup, picked up her list and, from there on the steps, began the reading of the names. It was a small list, only 357 names, and we would read it many times over the next two days while the quilt was on display. The eighteen panels of Proyecto Memorias looked lost in the center of the large square. What a contrast between this event and the last Names Project display we had attended in Washington, DC! There, the reading of the names went on for days without repetition—ten thousand in all—and the quilt panels, placed side by side, filled the entire Washington Mall.

In Havana, as the day wore on, volunteers dressed all in white maintained their positions on the edges of the fabric memorial with umbrellas opened against the relentless tropical sun. Several others moved quietly around the panels, straightening their borders and gently brushing them clean of leaves and twigs. William Tamayo's panel was there with his boxing gloves sewn into the center, and Alexei, an artist, was represented by a colorful mosaic and a poem. The panels were simple, sewn on thin white sheets of fabric, often inlaid with everyday items—-a favorite dress, some family photos, a cigarette package, a plastic spoon.

There had been no public announcement of this event—that was something the group had yet to achieve—but throughout the morning, people kept drifting in to view the quilt, drawn by the brightly colored panels and the crowd. The empty squares of white fabric we had placed at each corner began to fill with hand-written messages as people bent to record their thoughts and feelings. As I stopped to read what they had written, a small, thin boy standing next to me tugged at my arm, requesting one of the red ribbons we were giving away. As I pinned it on his shirt, he quietly confided, "My neighbor has AIDS. I'm sick too, with asthma. Sometimes I share my medicine with him."

By noon, the crowd had thinned a bit—people heading home to get out of the midday sun and complete the day's chores. A bus with tinted windows pulled up across the street and discharged a large group of camera-bedecked tourists chattering to each other in French. They drew curious stares from the Cuban crowd. The van from the sanatorium finally arrived with our lunch, and I took a break in the shade of a tree. My thoughts drifted back to the beginnings of this improbable project over a year ago.

"*Elena, favor de presentarse al frente.*" Alejandro's voice over the loudspeaker at the Capitolio pulled me back into the present. There were only a few people around the edges of the display as I took my place behind the microphone and began to read: *Orlando, Alexei, Norma, Niurka.* In a trembling voice I added the names of some of the kids I had cared for in my clinic in New Jersey . . . *Ella, Jasmine, Christina* . . . and then I spoke Clarence's name in a strong clear voice . . . and the names floated out into the air and over the quilt like runaway balloons lifting up and up into the sky.

Caridad called me over to greet her son, José, and we walked together to look at the panel she had painted for Orlando. The purple and orange orchid in the center blazed with color and love.

When it was time to close the display, we gathered up the remaining volunteers and began the closing ceremony that was conducted wherever the quilt was displayed. With volunteers at each corner of the quilt panels, we lifted them high into the air above our heads and slowly, silently walked around in a circle before returning them to the cement. Each panel was then folded gently into itself and the folded bundles were placed back in the center of the square.

We joined hands in a moment of respectful silence. As I looked around the circle, I couldn't help wondering which of my Cuban friends I might never see again. We had come together beyond the boundaries of our individual experience, beyond the borders of our two countries' conflicted history. Each of us could remember with painful clarity the exact moment that AIDS entered our life and changed it forever. Each of us had traveled so far from that moment to stand together on this day of remembrance under the burning Cuban sun.

Alejandro's niece and nephew point out an image
on the quilt that has caught their attention.

Onlookers stop to take in the first public display of Proyecto Memorias, the Cuban AIDS quilt, in front of the Cuban capitol. Many were moved to write a reflection.

EPILOGUE

DECEMBER 2016

The streets of Havana were eerily quiet as we drove from the airport to María Luisa's house: no couples smooching on the Malecón seawall, very few people on the streets, a hush over the whole city. The same 1940s and '50s cars traveled on the roadway as before, past the same revolutionary billboards, but also a few brand new hotels and shopping malls.

My goddaughter, Lucía, now a twenty-three-year-old student at Havana's prestigious Institute of Art, had met me at the airport. "Oye, Elena. *Escuche.* Do you hear how quiet it is? It has been like this for days. Even the dogs are not barking," she said as we made our way through the streets to the family apartment where I would stay for the eight days of my visit. "Wait till you see my room, Tía Elena," she said as she bumped my suitcase up the stairs. They had recently constructed a private room for Lucía out of a corner of the living room, and she was proudly turning it over to me.

María del Carmen, who had celebrated her ninetieth birthday that year with a party on the Malecón, greeted me at the door. "Ay, Elena. Come and see the funeral procession. They are taking his ashes to Santiago. They will pass through my hometown soon. It is so sad." Her eyes behind her thick glasses, forever broken and held together with tape, were moist with tears. Lucía shrugged her shoulders. It

was all a bit dramatic for her. Everyone knew he had to die sometime.
Nothing would really change.

It was December 5, 2016. I had arrived near the end of the *luto*,
the nine-day period of mourning for Cuba's revered leader, Fidel
Castro, who had died at the age of ninety on November 25th. Schools
were closed, theaters and cinemas were dark, no alcohol was being
sold, only skeleton crews were working in hospitals and factories.
Everything and everyone had stopped to mark Fidel's passing.

Of course, Lucía was right in a way. Fidel had been debilitated
for years, finally ceding the presidency to his brother Raul in 2008.
The CIA had tried to kill him numerous times in plots that included
exploding cigars, bacteria-infected scuba diving suits, and poisoned
pens. There were frequent rumors of his death, belied by rare public
appearances. But his presence loomed large throughout Cuba, Latin
America, and the world. I remembered racing past the reviewing
stand with thousands of others on May Day in 1996, hoping to catch
a glimpse of the man—tall, broad-shouldered, in his green medal-be-
decked uniform, waving at the crowds.

To honor Fidel's personal wishes, there had been no parade to
mark his death, no huge likenesses of him displayed in Revolution
Square, no body lying in state in the Capitolio—only a solemn procession of black cars, led by a military jeep towing an open trailer
bearing the simple pine box surrounded by white roses that held
Fidel's ashes. The procession was slowly making its way across the
island to Santiago de Cuba where he would be laid to rest, retracing
the rebel army's march across Cuba into Havana in 1959—the triumph of the revolution. Tens of thousands lined the streets along
the way, all ages, all races, five rows deep, waving small Cuban
flags.

We watched the TV for hours. The coverage doubled back to show
the throngs that had lined Revolution Square to bid farewell to their
leader several days earlier. Had María Luisa gone? Lucía and her

boyfriend? No, but they knew people who had—waiting in the sun to touch the pine box.

Footage of the procession was interrupted by clips of Cubans of every age, from every walk of life, from all the cities and small hamlets of the island, declaring *Yo Soy Fidel*—I am Fidel—in heartfelt interviews. Archival filmstrips of revolutionary battles, the literacy campaign, and Fidel's famously long speeches were repeated all day long. I had injured my knee schlepping my heavy suitcases on the journey and could barely walk, so I sat, leg propped up on a chair, bag of ice on my knee, glued to the TV as family members and neighbors came and went.

On the afternoon of the second day of my visit, María del Carmen, *una viejita* over ninety years old but still doing most of the shopping and cooking for the small family, returned from the market with a big grin on her face. "Mira Elenita," she said, "la piña!" In her hand sat a small fragrant pineapple, a treasure, elusive twenty years ago, that she had found at the farmer's market. What a feast we would have that night—*ensalada fria* with macaroni and pineapple, fresh fish, a bottle of wine—when I would meet María Luisa's new boyfriend for the first time (she had divorced Lucía's father years earlier). He was an actor like her, and a writer—older, worldly, unusually well-traveled for a Cuban.

Later we polished off a delicious dinner at the small round dining table with a plate of fresh fruit and espresso while the TV droned on in the background. After a second glass of wine, our conversation turned to politics—the uncertainty of future changes in Cuba, the growing anti-Trump protest movement in the US. "How could this have happened in your country?" Lucía's boyfriend asked the question on everyone's mind, the question we were still grappling with in New York. He was a young computer whiz and had broader access to the internet than most, so he had been following the news from the US.

Everyone listened in amazement as I described the huge angry demonstrations that had been taking place in large cities across the country—with Trump's inauguration still more than a month away. They had seen little coverage of this on their one nightly news station.

"Do you think Trump will change everything with Cuba back to the way it was? Will he undo all of Obama's policies?" María Luisa's boyfriend asked. I had described my trip here, so different from every other trip I had made to Cuba. I had purchased my plane tickets online with JetBlue, a direct flight from JFK Airport in New York, $200 round trip (I had checked that figure three times in disbelief), no license to apply for, only an online form asking me to check a box with the purpose of my trip—the choices so general as to be virtually meaningless: professional research, education, support for the Cuban people, cultural exchange. Baggage checked, boarding pass in hand with TSA PreCheck security designation, I'd relaxed, had a cup of coffee, and three hours later I was in Havana.

Oh, how much more challenging it had been just a few years earlier when I had to apply for a license from the Treasury Department for my trip, reserve an expensive charter flight months ahead of time, arrive in Miami the night before to depart at six the following morning, wait in a dark basement area of the airport with hundreds of anxious Cuban-Americans pulling behind them large plastic-wrapped suitcases filled with gifts and basic supplies for their family members, and then finally reach Cuba, only ninety miles from our shore, after two days of travel. Or the years before that, when I risked "illegal" trips, buying my ticket to Cuba in Cancún or Nassau and waiting nervously in the US customs line on the way back for the inevitable questions: "So, did you take any side trips while you were visiting the Bahamas?" "Did you spend the whole two weeks in Cancún?" How did they know? Was it written on my forehead? Once, only once, I made the mistake of answering "no" after the customs agent had strewn random clothing from my suitcase all over the conveyer belt with the irritated line behind me growing longer by the minute. "Oh, really," he had said, smiling and laying out the ticket stubs he had found among my dirty underwear. "How did you enjoy the National Theater in Havana?"

Would Trump roll back these changes in the US travel ban we were just beginning to enjoy? How would Raúl and the Cuban government navigate these new waters? And how would Cuba recover from the economic crisis brought on by the scarcity of petroleum from Venezuela, a vital trading partner dealing with its own crisis? None of us could know the future.

The next day my friend Alejandro from the Prevention Group and his partner, Antonio, paid me a visit. My knee was still swollen and painful, and their house was under construction again (rewiring and fixing up the patio), so our usual custom of sharing a meal with Alejandro's family would not happen during this visit. I loved Antonio dearly—he and Alejandro had been together for years, and I was happy that my friend had finally found his life partner. They were both still very involved in the activities of the Prevention Group and Proyecto Memorias, the AIDS Quilt project. Antonio worked at the Tropical Medicine Institute, but Alejandro had left to join the staff of Care Canada (he pronounced it Ka-rey). This gave him flexibility, a salary in dollars, the experience of traveling all over Cuba and Central America, and new skills as a project coordinator for agricultural initiatives—and he was loving it, though working very hard. During my visit the previous year, he had showed off the beehives on his patio, part of a project he was developing with Cuban farmers to encourage honey production. I had watched, fascinated, as he stood in front of his hive, holding the bees gently in the palm of his hand, unafraid of being stung because this was a particular kind of African bee that had no stinger. The descendants of the dachshunds I had met years earlier yapped and nipped at his feet.

"Y Mamá?" I asked, handing over the can of Bustelo coffee and bag of Lindor chocolate truffles I had brought for her. When I had asked Alejandro in an email what to bring her, he had replied, "Some chocolate and a *jaula*." I had to look up the unfamiliar word, which means cage, and took it to mean that his mother was still the strong, fiery woman I remembered.

We spent the afternoon catching up on other friends, on what was happening in the sanatorium, on the Quilt Project. Over the years, many friends, both staff and patients from the sanatorium, had left Cuba. Gone were the days when this would be discussed in hushed conversation and would bring shame and worry on the family left behind. Cubans leaving the island were no longer "traitors" betraying the revolution, but, like other émigrés, simply people seeking a better life and more or different opportunities. So we updated our list. Jaime, whose house had served as the incubator for Proyecto Memorias, was living in Florida. So, too, were Chavela and Manolo, the creative team of health educators who had inspired me when we did our first training. They had moved to be close to their daughters, who had left some years before, and their grandchildren.

Dr. Jorge Pérez, the courageous director of the sanatorium who fought tirelessly for a more humane AIDS policy in the early days, was now the Director of the IPK—the Institute for Tropical Medicine—and showed no signs of slowing down. He had been depicted in a mainstream, well-received Cuban film called *Boleto al Paraiso* (*Ticket to Paradise*), which tells the story of a group of young Cubans who injected themselves with HIV-tainted blood to win entry into the sanatorium where they thought they could live a more secure and comfortable life. I had seen the film a few years earlier at a festival in New York. The story had brought back memories of Roberto, the gentle father and artist, who had first opened my eyes to the reality of this choice, one that he himself had made, self-injecting to join his sister in the sanatorium in search of emotional support at a difficult time in his life. I had met that sister, Ophelia, in 2012 when

I was invited to facilitate a workshop for Proyecto Memorias at the sanatorium. She was still living there, doing well, coordinating the project in Havana. After the workshop, we displayed the quilt at a local park. The ritual of unfolding the fabric panels, lifting them high into the air, and placing them lovingly on the ground still held so much power and memory for me. Ophelia had shown me the panel she had made for Roberto after his death a few years earlier, with the quote from José Martí he had shared with me the last time we met: "Man doesn't learn from the times he falls down, but from the times he picks himself up."

I had reconnected with Tanya, the *friki* poet, during that 2012 visit as well. No more blonde spiky hair and crotch-high shorts for her. Tanya was a grandmother now and looked like a very respectable Cuban woman of a certain age. Her nervous laugh still appeared at intervals, and she was still writing poetry and living in the sanatorium. I don't know if that was by choice or if she had never been granted permission to leave because of her conduct, but she seemed relaxed and content with her life. Alejandro had told me that, ironically, the government was now trying to close the sanatoriums for economic reasons, and the people who relied on them, who lived in them, were fighting to keep them open.

"Y Hermes?" Alejandro called from Lucía's bedroom where she was showing off the décor. Lucía was a painter, but at the Art Institute she studied theatrical design, and she had applied her skills to her tiny, carefully decorated bedroom.

"*Hermes está bien. Trabajando. Gordo.*" Hermes was well, working, and fat (meaning healthy), I told Alejandro. Hermes, whose father, the *comandante* of the revolution, had made it impossible to leave Cuba for years, had finally left for good in 2007. After years of trying and being denied, he had been granted a visa to attend an AIDS conference in New York, staying with me in my studio apartment on the Upper West Side. He hoped to travel back to Cuba via Miami to visit his mother, but that request was denied. I remembered a sleepless night of watching him pace and smoke and cry and pace—and then finally decide that he was going to Miami anyway. He could not leave the US without seeing his mother.

Hermes never returned to Cuba. He stayed in Florida for several years until he tired of the conservative, right-wing Cuban community there. Hermes may have left Cuba, but he still loved his country and recognized many of the positive changes the revolution had brought. He moved to Washington, DC, where he lived on a tree-lined block of art deco buildings that reminded him of Vedado in Havana.

A couple of years earlier, María Antonia, the psychologist from the sanatorium who had been my supervisor, also left Cuba and found an apartment in the same building. They now had a little expat Cuban colony growing there, and when I visited, we all gathered in Hermes's pleasant apartment for a meal and some reminiscing. Hermes was working as a peer counselor at the Clinica del Pueblo, a clinic that served Washington's low-income Latino community of Central American immigrants. Unlike the mostly undocumented immigrants he worked with, Hermes, like most Cubans, had applied for and been granted political asylum under the US policy called "wet foot, dry foot" that welcomed any Cuban who was able to place one foot on US soil. Cubans "fleeing communism" by risking drowning and death on rafts made for effective propaganda, even though mostly what they were fleeing was the lack of economic opportunity on the island.

For the first years of his self-imposed exile, Hermes, like other Cubans who left, was barred from returning to Cuba. But that, too, had changed and he now returned regularly to visit his family there, even his ailing father whose severe presence had loomed over his life for so long.

"Pero dime algo de tu vida, Elena," Alejandro said. "We're talking about everyone else but you haven't said anything about yourself.

How's Paul? How are Angelica and Camilo? Tell me about your other grandkids." I took a deep breath. Where to begin? Alejandro and Antonio had met my life partner, Paul, the previous year when I'd finally persuaded him to accompany me to Cuba and meet the "Cuban family" who were so important to me. And they had long been following the ups and downs of my kids' and now grandkids' lives. Alejandro had even visited us once in Brooklyn, coming down on the Greyhound bus from Boston where he was participating in a fellowship program at Harvard.

"Everyone's good. The kids are growing. Paul is playing his accordion at all the protest marches." I had met Paul, a lawyer and musician, online in 2000 when I finally felt ready to commit to a long-term relationship, and we had been together ever since, buying and fixing up an old house, now both semi-retired but busy with things we loved to do—music for him, writing for me, and fighting for social justice for both.

My daughter, Angelica, who had brought us fabric to start the quilt and the infamous *pene de goma*, the life-like rubber penis that was still in use for condom demos, was now a mother herself—of my grandson, Camilo, named in part for the Cuban revolutionary and close confidante to Fidel whose small plane mysteriously disappeared in 1959. Angelica's name had also been born in Cuba where I had met her father, Victor. We had chosen to name her for a dear friend, a fellow brigadista on the Venceremos Brigade who died in a car accident shortly after our return.

My son, Jonah, had married and had three small children whose primary language was Spanish (their mother was Argentinean) and who corrected their *abuela* when she mispronounced or misspoke. And Clarence's daughter, Kiwan, was a grandmother already, living with her three sons in South Carolina and following in the footsteps of her optimistic, energetic activist father.

"I'm not working for MEDICC anymore," I told them. For the

previous several years I had been working with an organization dedicated to promoting health exchange between Cuba and the US—a
perfect part-time job that allowed me to renew my love affair with
Cuba every six months and see the island with a fresh lens when I
led tours for groups of residents from a community health project in
the South Bronx. That project had ended and, though I was still in
contact with various community health groups, I was happy not to
have a demanding job anymore. This trip, my first personal visit in a
long time, had given me the opportunity to spend unhurried hours
with friends. When my knee improved, I was still hoping to do some
exploring and traveling.

"We've got to get going, Elenita," Alejandro said, getting up
from the couch and beginning a round of kisses and good-byes.
It was Saturday, and they needed to do some errands for Mama
and get ready for the work week ahead. We turned our attention
back to the TV where they were replaying Fidel's interment, which
had taken place that morning. We watched as the Jeep carrying
Fidel's remains traveled the final distance to the Santa Ifigenia
Cemetery, where other heroes of the Cuban Revolution, including
José Martí, were buried. In an ending that could have been written
by one of Cuba's masters of ironic cinema, the Russian-made jeep
had broken down and had to be pushed into the cemetery by a
group of soldiers.

A small group, including Raúl, Fidel's wife, and several of his children, as well as a few Cuban and foreign dignitaries, laid his remains
to rest in a brief private ceremony The urn was carried by Fidel's wife
to a large granite mausoleum next to the tomb of Martí, fashioned
from a boulder extracted from the earth of his small home town east
of Santiago. The ashes were slipped into the stone by Raúl, and the
mausoleum was sealed with a plaque saying simply "Fidel." In keeping with Fidel's wishes that there be no cult of personality following
his death, the Cuban legislature had enacted a law prohibiting the

use of his name on monuments, statues, plazas, streets, or cultural institutions—and there would be no Fidel branding of commercial products or advertising.

On Sunday, the mourning period officially ended, and my knee felt better, so Lucía and I decided to go shopping. We took a *maquina*—one of the unique Cuban taxis, usually a 1940s-era Ford or Chevy, that picked up passengers along a fixed route until not one more could squeeze in and charged just a few cents to get you close to where you were going. We headed down to Calle Obispo, the main pedestrian street in Old Havana, so I could pick up a few small gifts for family and friends. The cobblestone walkway was jammed with groups of tourist and Cuban families feeling the release from the restrictions of the last two weeks, but there was still an unfamiliar quiet in the air.

This was the street I had walked down so often to visit my beloved amiga Caridad in her small apartment on Calle Amistad in a crumbling neighborhood of central Havana. I remembered the last time as I walked with Lucía beside me.

"Mamashka!" Caridad had greeted me with the nickname she and Alejandro had given me when they learned that my grandparents were from Russia. "Do you still have the *chancleta*?" she had asked with a little smile, brandishing a blue rubber bathroom slipper in her hand.

On my trip the year before, I had stayed with her for a few days and left this slipper behind in her bedroom. Caridad suggested that we each keep one of the pair to remind us of each other when we were apart. "*Si seguro, la tengo.* It's safe in my closet at home."

I had to work hard to keep the shock I felt at seeing my old friend so wan and thin from showing on my face. She had been battling ovarian cancer for the past two years, and it was back—a spot on her liver and one near her pancreas. She would have to start chemo again. "*Yo soy fuerte,* I'm a strong woman, Elena, and I want to go on.

I've lived so long with this virus, longer than anyone thought. But I'm worried about the cancer. What if my body can't fight anymore?"

I had no answer . . . only sadness that my dear friend had yet another challenge to face in a life that had already presented so many.

"Hasta la proxima, amiga." Till the next time. Caridad waved the slipper at me as I left. But I felt sure that I would never see her again.

I got the news weeks after Caridad died. I was teaching AIDS educators in rural Tanzania for the summer, miles from the internet and my email. Alejandro wrote and told me, attaching a tribute he had written to *"Nuestra Paloma* (Our Dove), a woman who demonstrated love and tenderness confronting all the difficulties of her life." I cried in my cot in the dark Tanzanian night and returned to teach my class in the morning, determined to honor my friend in my work and life. The blue *chancleta* remained in my closet and remains there still, waiting and yearning for its partner.

Lucía and I continued our walk. I found an unusual pair of maracas I thought Paul would like and some Spanish children's books for Jonah's kids. Camilo would have to be content with yet another T-shirt. At the end of the cobbled block dotted with souvenir shops and small cafés loomed the Capitolio, the Capitol building, its dome shrouded in scaffolding from a long renovation project. It was in front of this building, twenty years earlier, that we had unfolded the quilt for the first time and launched Proyecto Memorias. I felt both proud and melancholy: proud of all that we had accomplished, of being a small part of Cuba's largely successful effort to keep the AIDS epidemic at bay, of enduring friendships, and yet surrounded by the memories of those who were no longer with us—Clarence, Orlando, Roberto, Diego the tailor, Caridad.

"Que te pasa, tia Elena?" What's wrong, Lucía asked, shaking my

shoulder gently and guiding me past a large pothole in the street. *Nada*. Nothing, I said, nothing, my heart suddenly filled with gratitude and love.

"I'm good," I said.

And I was.

I am.

I continue to return to Cuba at least once a year, to work with Proyecto Memorias, renew old friendships, visit my family and soak in the strength and resilience of this generous island.

*In May of 2019, Cleve Jones, the founder of the AIDS Memorial Quilt,
visited Cuba. Panels from the U.S. Quilt were hung at the offices
of the Cuban National Center for Sexual Education (Cenesex) and
Proyecto Memorias was unfolded at Los Cocos in a moving ceremony.*

ACKNOWLEDGMENTS

I have worked on this book, on and off, for the last twenty years, and I couldn't possibly have persevered without the love, support, and expertise of so many. To all who asked a challenging question or offered a word of encouragement along the way, I send my heartfelt thanks.

To the folks named below—family, friends, compañeros(as), and fellow writers—I am grateful beyond words, but will try to find a few.

To Paulie, the best compañero, one-man cheerleading squad, and punctuation detective a self-doubting writer could ask for. Our late in life, non-traditional romance has given me wings. Rest up and get ready for my novel!

To my "kids" now grown—Jonah, Angelica, and Kiwan—who rose to so many occasions with strength and humor. I am so grateful for the wonderful adults you have grown into and for your patient understanding and love.

To my brother Rick, my role model for embracing life with all its ups and downs and living it to the fullest, and who is also one of my writing mentors. And to Val, who has brought so much strength and joy to my brother and our whole family.

To the big, loving Fitch family that welcomed me so warmly and has always kept me close. Keeping Clarence alive in our hearts has created a bond that will last a lifetime.

To the Gold-Zelermyer clan, who drew me in and saw me through with love and acceptance—especially my dear friend Tami whose matchmaking brought me and Clarence together, and who always asked so many questions that I had no choice but to write a book. Thanks for that and for *Another Brother*, the powerful film that continues to tell Clarence's story.

And to the Stein/Israel family, many thanks for your support and encouragement.

To Greg P., who was like a brother to our dear Clarence and who has become a loving guide for me—along with Donna, whose gentle spirit continues to inspire me.

To my sister-friends Karen W., Maryellen, Kay, Maritza, and Pam, who read early drafts, encouraged me to keep going, and convinced me that I had a story worth telling.

To Darlene G., with whom I have found an enduring friendship and an (almost) daily writing practice that has improved and enriched my writing and my life . . . prompt by prompt.

To the intrepid Hundred Worders—Annalee, Ellen, Catherine, JoAnn, Stu, and Brian—eight years still strong and going. For a few years there, a hundred words a week was all I could find, but it was enough.

To Mindy Lewis, my incomparable first writing teacher and mentor who started me down this path, offered invaluable feedback in her gentle way, and believed that this book would be published someday. You were right!

To the NY Writers Coalition—I'm so glad I found this writing community. Our mission of bringing writing to the most marginalized in New York City and our mantra that "everyone who writes is a writer" continue to nurture my growth as a writer and activist. And to the amazing writers of my 14th St. Y workshop—your honesty and dedication to returning each week to write your stories nourishes and sustains me.

To SheWrites.com, who created a community of women writers

and named me as a finalist in their Passion Project contest at a time when I most needed this shot of encouragement, and to She Writes Press, especially the fearless and groundbreaking Brooke Warner, for creating a publishing platform for women writers and walking me through this process with so much grace. Special thanks to Joan Dempsey, my developmental editor, who understood my effort to find a structure that worked and helped me get there, and to Jennifer Caven, who made the copy-editing process so painless. Thanks also to She Writes Press project managers, Cait Levin and Shannon Green, and cover designer, Julie Metz. To my publicists, Ellen Whitfield, Marissa DeCuir, and the staff at JKS Publications, who partnered with me to ensure that this book would find its audience.

To the compañeros and compañeras I worked with in Cuba—Dr. Jorge Pérez, María Antonia Alfonso, Isabela "Chavela" Duque and her husband Manolo—and all of the patients and workers who shared their stories with me and helped me understand. Thank you for inviting me in to experience both the triumphs and frustrations of your work.

To Diane Appelbaum, MEDICC, and the dedicated community activists all around the US who give life to the word "solidarity" in their work with the Community Partnerships for Health Equity (CPHE) . . . and a special shout out to the passionate folk at Claremont Village who welcomed me warmly and stuck around long enough to find out what this exchange with Cuba was all about.

And to the Cuban family who has fed me, dried my tears, showed me how to navigate the unfamiliar waters of life in Havana, laughed at my Spanish *faux pas* and always welcomed me back—*mil gracias por todo*: Ana Gloria, Anita and Rocio, Mama, Norma Guillard, María Eugenia y Maravillas de la Infancia, Conner Gorry and the staff at Cuba Libro, Carlitos y Aramis de Cirhabana Cirkus, and all the friendly faces and generous guides whose names I don't remember or never knew.

To all my coworkers at the Children's Hospital AIDS Program (CHAP) in Newark, New Jersey. We were in the trenches, but we knew how to laugh. I'll never forget AZT and the Side Effects, and all of the beautiful children we cared for together.

And most especially and from the bottom of my heart—to the members of Grupo de Prevención SIDA (GPSIDA) in Havana, Cuba. We stitched a quilt together and created Proyecto Memorias—and friendships that have only grown stronger through losses, distance, and changing times: Carlos, Joel, Jorge, Armando, Mayda, Raul . . and those who left us too soon . . . Tomas, María Julia, Ricardo, Myriam, Emilio. and many more.

And finally, for my dad, Arnie Schwolsky, a mensch and a helluva writer of letters to the editor. I promised you a story, not this one exactly, but here it is . . .

And for you, dear readers, who have plucked this book off the shelf or downloaded it from the web and taken it home: I hope the stories from *Waking in Havana* open the window to a new world, as they did for me.

CHRONOLOGY OF GLOBAL AIDS EPIDEMIC

Cuba milestones in italics

1981: Cases of a rare pneumonia (PCP) and a rare form of cancer (Kaposi's Sarcoma) diagnosed in previously healthy young gay men in California and New York.

1982: The new disease becomes known as Gay-Related Immunodeficiency Disease (GRID). Cases also diagnosed in hemophiliacs, Haitians, and IV-drug users

1983: Retrovirus identified as cause of disease. First cases reported in children and women who were sexual partners of infected men. Major routes of transmission identified and casual contact, food, air, water, and surface transmission ruled out.

Cuba becomes aware of and concerned about emerging disease; Ministry of Public Health (MINSAP) establishes a National AIDS Commission.

Cuba destroys and bans all imported blood products and begins testing all donated blood.

1984: Blood test to detect presence of virus developed. Scientists hope for vaccine within two years.

1985: *First case of HIV in Cuba clinically diagnosed. Initial cases discovered in soldiers who had traveled back from service in Angola.*

First commercial blood test licensed. US blood-supply screening begins.

First International AIDS Conference held. Every region in the world reports at least one case.

1986: *Cuban National Program for the Prevention and Control of HIV/AIDS launched.*

The first AIDS sanatorium opens in Havana. All Cubans who test positive for HIV are mandated to live in a sanatorium. Eventually there will be one in each province.

Cuban government announces publicly that HIV infection has been detected in the population.

First Cuban dies of AIDS-related complications.

Eighty-five countries report a total of 38,401 cases.

1987: The World Health Organization launches the Global Program to Fight AIDS.

Zidovudine (AZT) is approved as monotherapy for AIDS patients in Cuba and the world.

1988: First World AIDS Day is celebrated on December 1st. The US reports 100,000 cases.

1989: *First case of pediatric HIV detected in Cuba.*

1990: US immigration policy bars people with HIV from entering country to attend 6th International AIDS Conference.

US reports 307,000 cases.

Eight to ten million cases reported worldwide.

1991: *AIDS Prevention Group (GPSIDA) officially established in Cuba.*

Red Ribbon becomes international symbol of the fight against AIDS.

Magic Johnson reveals that he is HIV positive.

Freddie Mercury, lead singer of Queen, reveals he has AIDS and dies the next day.

1992: First rapid test for HIV is developed.

Arthur Ashe reveals he has AIDS, acquired from a blood transfusion.

The International AIDS Conference is moved from Boston to Amsterdam to protest US immigration policy.

1993: *Cuban mandatory sanatorium policy amended to allow alternative known as the Ambulatory Care System.*

People testing positive for HIV no longer have to live in the sanitoria but can live, work, study and receive medical attention in their home communities.

1994: First Oral HIV test is developed.

AZT is used to prevent mother to child transmission of the virus.

1995: *Cuban Laboratories begin using Cuban-manufactured HIV test kits nationwide.*

A new line of drugs (protease inhibitors) prove highly effective in treating HIV/AIDS, resulting in a 60 to 80 percent decrease in deaths.

1996 : *Cuban children with HIV and their mothers begin receiving antiretroviral treatment.*

Cuba joins the International NAMES (AIDS QUILT) Project.

UNAIDS, the Joint United Nations Programme on HIV/AIDS, is

formed, uniting the efforts of 11 UN organizations to fight AIDS worldwide.

Optimism grows about AIDS treatment in the developed world, but advanced treatment remains prohibitively expensive in sub-Saharan Africa where epidemic is growing exponentially.

23 million infected worldwide.

1997: *Pregnant women with HIV in Cuba begin receiving AZT to prevent mother-to-child transmission.*

1998: *Cuba's ambulatory care system for people living with HIV/AIDS is significantly expanded.*

Cuban National STI/HIV/AIDS Prevention Center opens.

Cuban Support Line (Línea de Apoyo) network for people with HIV/ AIDS founded.

2000: *Cuban project for men who have sex with men (Proyecto HSH) created.*

2001: *Cuba begins manufacturing its own antiretroviral drugs and distributing them free to those needing them.*

Cuban National STI/HIV/AIDS Strategic Plan 2001–2006 launched.

2003: *Universal antiretroviral treatment achieved in Cuba.*

Cuba receives award from the Global Fund to Fight AIDS, Tuberculosis, and Malaria.

2005: *Cuban Ministry of Public Health further refines Sanatoria Care and Ambulatory Care Systems.*

2013: *Cuba is declared the first country to completely eliminate mother-to-child transmission of HIV by the PanAmerican Health Organization (PAHO).*

Current Statistics (2018)**

Global: 37.9 million people are currently living with HIV/AIDS, 74.9 million have been infected since the start of the epidemic, and 32 million have died.

Cuba: Out of a population of 11 million, 31,000 adults and <100 children are currently living with HIV/AIDS. Approximately 72% of all HIV infected Cubans and 95% of all HIV-infected pregnant women receive anti-retroviral therapy. Less than 500 Cubans have died since the start of the epidemic.

*Source for Cuban data: Oxfam International, Cuba's HIV/AIDS Strategy: An Integrated, Rights-Based Approach

**Source for 2018 Data: UNAIDS Data Report 2019.

APPENDIX II

TO LEARN MORE . . .

Cuba-US Relations & History

Cuba and the United States: A Chronological History, Jane Franklin, Ocean Press, 1997.

Cruel and Unusual Punishment: The US Blockade Against Cuba, Mary Murray, Ocean Press, 1993.

Venceremos Brigade: Young Americans Sharing the Life and Work of Revolutionary Cuba, Simon and Schuster, 1971.

Cuba-U.S. Relations: Obama and Beyond, Arnold August, Fernwood Publishing, 2017.

Un Año Sin Domingos/A Year Without Sundays: Images from the Literacy Campaign in Cuba, Catherine Murphy & Carlos Torres Cairo, Ediciones Aurelia, 2018.

Cuban Revelations: Behind The Scenes In Havana, Marc Frank, University Press of Florida, 2013.

Health Care & HIV/AIDS

Healing the Masses: Cuban Health Politics at Home and Abroad, Julie M. Feinsilver, Univ. of California Press, 1993.

SIDA: Confesiones a un Médico & Nuevas Confesiones a un Médico, Jorge Perez Avila, Casa Editora Abril, 2006 & 2011.

MEDICC Review, www.mediccreview.org.

A doctor and his patients talk about AIDS in Cuba, Jorge Pérez Avila, Casa Editora Abril, 2015.

Travel, Culture and Everyday Life

100 Places In Cuba Every Woman Should Go, Conner Gorry, Travelers' Tales, Solas House, 2018.

Conversations with Cuba, C. Peter Ripley, University of Georgia Press, 1999.

Trading with the Enemy: A Yankee Travels Through Castro's Cuba, Tom Miller, Atheneum Books, 1992.

Bridges to Cuba, Puestes a Cuba: Cuban and Cuban-American artists, writers and scholars explore identity, nationality, and homeland, Ruth Behar, editor, University of Michigan Press, 1995.

An Island Called Home: Returning to Jewish Cuba, Ruth Behar, Rutgers University Press, 2007.

Havana Without Makeup: Inside the Soul of the City, Herman Portocarero, Turtle Point Press, 2017.

Burnt Sugar: Contemporary Cuban Poetry in English and Spanish, edited by Lori Marie Carlson and Oscar Hijuelos, Free Press, 2006.

Telex from Cuba: A Novel, Rachel Kushner, Scribner, 2008.

King of Cuba: A Novel, Cristina Garcia, Scribner, 2013.

Films

El Acompañante (*The Companion*), 2015, Amazon Prime.

Habanastation (*Havana Station*), 2011, Cinequest.

Boleto al Paraiso (*Ticket to Paradise*), 2010, Vimeo.

Viva Cuba (*Long Live Cuba*), 2005, Amazon Prime.

Guantanamera, 1997, Amazon Prime.

Fresa Y Chocolate (Strawberry & Chocolate), 1993, Netflix.

Salud! What puts Cuba on the map in the quest for global health, Connie Field, 2006 www.saludthefilm.net.

Another Brother, a documentary film by Tami Gold, 1998, Vimeo, Third World Newsreel.

Maestra, a documentary film by Catherine Murphy, 2012, Women Make Movies.

The AIDS Epidemic in the U.S. & the World
The Early Years

And The Band Played On: Politics, People, and the AIDS Epidemic, Randy Shilts, St. Martin's Press, 1987.

My Own Country: A Doctor's Story, Abraham Verghese, Vintage Books, 1994.

Heaven's Coast: a memoir, Mark Doty, Harper Perennial, 1996.

AIDS Activism

Stitching a Revolution: The Making of an Activist, Cleve Jones and Jeff Dawson, HarperOne, 2000.

When We Rise: My Life in the Movement, Cleve Jones, Hatchette, 2017.

How to Survive a Plague: The Story of how Activists and Scientists Tamed AIDS, David France, Vintage Books, 2017.

The Quilt: Stories from the Names Project, Cindy Ruskin, Pocket Books, 1988.

The Global Epidemic

Infections and Inequalities: The Modern Plagues, Paul Farmer, University of California Press, 1999.

AIDS And Accusation: Haiti and the Geography of Blame, Paul Farmer, University of California Press, 1992.

28 Stories of AIDS in Africa, Stephanie Nolen, Walker & Co., 2007.

Hidden in the Blood: A Personal Investigation of AIDS in the Yucatån, Carter Wilson, Columbia University Press, 1995.

Positive Women: Voices of Women Living with AIDS, Edited by Andrea Rudd and Darien Taylor, Second Story Press, 1992.

ABOUT THE AUTHOR

© Resa Sunshine Photography

Elena Schwolsky, RN, MPH is a nurse, community health educator, activist, and writer who spent a decade as a pediatric nurse at the height of the AIDS epidemic. She has trained AIDS educators in Cuba and Tanzania, and currently teaches community health workers in diverse urban neighborhoods in New York City. Her essays have appeared in *The American Journal of Nursing* and *The Veteran*, and her work has been included in the anthologies *Storied Dishes: What Our Family Recipes Tell Us About Who We Are and Where We've Been* and *Reflections on Nursing: 80 inspiring stories on the art and science of nursing*. A chapter she cowrote appears in the textbook *Children, Families and AIDS: Psychosocial and Therapeutic Issues*. Schwolsky is the recipient of an award from the Barbara Deming Money for Women Fund and is proud to be recognized as the *madrina* (godmother) of Proyecto Memorias, the Cuban AIDS Quilt project.

SELECTED TITLES FROM SHE WRITES PRESS

She Writes Press is an independent publishing company founded to serve women writers everywhere. Visit us at www.shewritespress.com.

Renewable: One Woman's Search for Simplicity, Faithfulness, and Hope by Eileen Flanagan $16.95, 978-1-63152-968-9

At age forty-nine, Eileen Flanagan had an aching feeling that she wasn't living up to her youthful ideals or potential, so she started trying to change the world—and in doing so, she found the courage to change her life.

Home Free: Adventures of a Child of the Sixties by Rifka Kreiter $16.95, 978-1631521768

A memoir of a young woman's passionate quest for liberation—one that leads her out of the darkness of a fraught childhood and through Manhattan nightclubs, broken love affairs, and virtually all the political and spiritual movements of the sixties.

Naked Mountain: A Memoir by Marcia Mabee $16.95, 978-1-63152-097-6

A compelling memoir of one woman's journey of natural world discovery, tragedy, and the enduring bonds of marriage, set against the backdrop of a stunning mountaintop in rural Virginia.

Miracle at Midlife: A Transatlantic Romance by Roni Beth Tower $16.95, 978-1-63152-123-2

An inspiring memoir chronicling the sudden, unexpected, and life-changing two-year courtship between a divorced American lawyer living on a houseboat in the center of Paris and an empty-nested clinical psychologist living in Connecticut.

Godmother: An Unexpected Journey, Perfect Timing, and Small Miracles by Odile Atthali $16.95, 978-1-63152-172-0

After thirty years of traveling the world, Odile Atthalin—a French intellectual from a well-to-do family in Paris—ends up in Berkeley, CA, where synchronicities abound and ultimately give her everything she has been looking for, including the gift of becoming a godmother.